YOU CAN'T SLEEP HERE:

A CLOWN'S GUIDE TO SURVIVING HOMELESSNESS

D1733537

ROBIN RAY

You Can't Sleep Here – A Clown's Guide To Surviving
Homelessness
Copyright © 2016 by Robin Ray
https://seattlewordsmith.wordpress.com/

I have tried to recreate events, locales and conversations from my memories of them. In order to maintain their anonymity in some instances I have changed the names of individuals and places, I may have changed some identifying characteristics and details such as physical properties, occupations and places of residence.

"All the world's a stage, and all the men and women merely players."

William Shakespeare

"All the world's a stage, except for the homeless, where it's mostly a place of refuge and surrender."

Robin Ray

OTHER BOOKS *by* ROBIN RAY

Tears *of a* Clown
Murder *in* Rock & Roll Heaven
Stranded *in* Paradise
Wetland *&* Other Stories
Commoner *the* Vagabond

Table *of* Contents

INTRODUCTION

I'M SITTING comfortably in my adopted library, in my adopted hometown of sunny Seattle, creating this guidebook. It's a balmy 65 degrees outside with just a sprinkle of spring rain dampening the air. Being the poor bloke that I am, I'm basically attired in hand-me-downs. My shoes, Timberlands, were a donation as was my red t-shirt, chequered, long-sleeved pullover, and a pair of black pants that wouldn't look out of place in a Catholic Boys' Seminary. A few hours ago, while waiting for this library to open, I sat outside, near the sidewalk, feeding the pigeons a few crackers I'd acquired from the local food bank this week. Nourishing the birds warms my heart. Their beaks aren't supple enough to bend into a Cheshire smile, but I can tell from their excitability that they're pleased by my altruism. I doubt they understand that I get more from feeding them than they do from pecking up my crumbs, but that doesn't matter. We're kindred spirits helping each other to do that one thing which keeps us in perpetuity – survive.

Homelessness is one of those unfortunate disasters no one hopes they get, like skin cancer, ringworms, or an airplane fuselage falling through their living room while they're in their bedroom making whoopee. I'm sure if I went around the country asking people about their thoughts on homelessness, I'll probably hear things like, "I'd rather have my nuts slammed in a door than be homeless," or "I'd rather go blind than be homeless" or "I'd rather drink bleach for a week than be homeless." I mean, that's a little drastic, don't you think? Drink bleach for a week? Who could last drinking bleach for even ¼ of a day? That just goes to show how much disdain people have for homelessness.

Yet, there they are. People sleeping on the street. People sleeping in parks. People sleeping in train stations. People sleeping in bus stations. People sleeping in airport terminals, staircases, roofs, vestibules, entryways, chimneys (don't ask), parking lots, church basements, public benches, abandoned factories, beaches, woods, forests and jungles, practically anywhere they can stretch themselves out horizontally for an hour or two. The federal definition of homelessness, being relatively broad, also includes those who stay in hotels and motels paid for by the government or charitable institutions as well as shelters, transitional shelters and single room occupancies. It's a sad commentary, really, but there it is, as real as the red on a baboon's behind.

For as long as I can remember, I've always been homeless. Sure, there were spurts where I did have a roof over my head, but those were always short lived. As kids, we moved around a lot. Today, occupying the couch of a forgotten cousin; tomorrow, sharing the porch of a sympathetic neighbor with the neighborhood drunks. Naturally, I couldn't make or keep friends while transitory like that. In fact, I'm surprised I even learned how to read and write. You'd think from being itinerant, the only thing I'd learn was never cling steadfastly to anything because, well, it'd be gone faster than a politician's word. At least that uncertain, nomadic, difficult type of life did make you tough. There's no way you'd get angry if a dinner host neglected to give you dessert at a cotillion because you'd be too grateful just for a simple morsel to eat in the first place.

Not one day goes by without you hearing about the plight and difficulties of the homeless. All the civil and religious wars around the world contribute to creating more and more refugees, homeless people, every day. They seek any port in their storms but are invariably turned away due to there being way too many desperate ones like them. The destitute reach out to governments, foreign and domestic, for assistance, but often receive very little or no help at all. Churches, mosques, synagogues and temples throw their doors open from time to time, yet these institutions sometimes do have to turn multitudes away because they ran out of bread or soup or mats for sleeping on. Worldly institutions like the Red Cross, FEMA and Catholic Charities are there to lend a helping hand, but sometimes they get so embroiled in such deep inter-governmental bureaucracy that the very ones they seek to help often get left standing out in the cold, often neglected, often forgotten.

Homelessness can happen to anyone, unless you're Bill Gates. He's worth $70 Billion. Even if he rented a crackhead motel room in a seedy part of town for $65 a night, it'd still take him about a billion years to run out of money, less if he patronized the fast-talking, one-toothed, meth-addicted hookers just outside his window. Still, though, even if Brother Gates lost 1/1,000,000 of his cash, he wouldn't be related to the status of the underclass, the Untouchables, as it were. Yes, the caste system exists in America. Let's not pretend that it doesn't. It's not a blood thing, either. I'm an Untouchable yet I have a brother who's a doctor so he was able to shimmy himself into the upper classes, the Brahmin. Yuppies are Brahmin; hipsters, who sit just one caste below the yuppies, can go either way. If hipsters, or millenials as they're called these days, work hard and put in the extra hours, they can wedge their way in with the Brahmin sect. One misstep, though, and they're out here on the sidewalk with the rest of us beggars.

There are many, many reasons why people end up hitting the skids – drug and alcohol addiction, fires, floods, earthquakes, tsunamis and other natural disasters, wars, corporate downsizing, rents rising, divorces, job loss, mental health, carelessness, heading out to Nashville with your guitar to become a country music star or busing to Hollywood with a pocketful of glossies to be a movie star, kissing your hard-earned money goodbye in a casino, marrying some young tart who promises you the world then cleans you out of house and home when your back is turned, etc. The list is as endless as the worries and wrath you incur. Pitiful. Probably the only industry that benefits from your downfall is the porn industry as most people would do anything for a buck, even if that means dressing up like Tarzan in high heels and swinging your half-naked ass around the nearest greased-up pole for $10 and a fifth of cheap vodka.

Crime and poverty and homelessness go hand in hand, like prunes, toilets and diarrhea. America's Age of Depression had to have been one of the worst times in history. Poor children were sold out to rich neighbors like lemonade. Backyard abortions were as common as pigeon poop in an Italian plaza. Bank robberies were the everyday norm. Bread lines stretched on for blocks and blocks. At least you could get a shave and a haircut for two bits, and a plate of ham and eggs from a diner for ten cents, but even that was too costly for some folks. There's a historical hotel here in Pioneer Square in downtown Seattle that still has an outdoor sign that reflects America's glorious past – 'Hotel Rooms, 75 cents.' Not bad, really, but I'm sure even scraping together 75 cents back then was like pulling teeth because, even today, you can still go downtown and be hard-pressed to find a homeless person who has at least 75 cents in his or her pocket.

I used to have a saying: The wealth of a city is determined by the depth of its arts. I still believe that, but I also think the wealth of a city is determined by the health of its people, and if some of the people can see their ribs beneath their tattered clothes or the lines of sleepless nights beneath their bloodshot eyes, how healthy is the city, really? If anything, poverty is but a study in contrasts. On any given day, you can see Llewellyn Van Yuppie walking her furry, white $4000 shih tzu right next to Broke Ass Benny catching 40 winks on a metal bench in the midtown bus stop. Right down the block, there's Hopeless Harry with his dirty palms pressed against the pristine glass wall of Le Elite Bistro, his bulging eyes fixed on the steamy, decadently square plates of duck confit and moules frites sitting lovingly between Mr. & Mrs. Made It Big. And right around the corner, just outside the recently-renovated Red Carpet Theatre, Penniless Paula is begging for nickels and dimes from the black-tie crowd who paid for seats with more money than Paula ever made in four months flipping burgers at the greasy spoon down on Desolation Boulevard.

So, what is a poor sucker to do when the carpet gets yanked out from beneath his feet, when he comes home to find an eviction noticed nailed to his front door? Some people make a beeline to the highest bridge in town and just say, "Fuck it. I'm done. Goodbye Cruel World. It's Been Real." Some people make a beeline straight to their favorite house of worship and pray earnestly for help. Some get on the phone and call every Tom, Dick and Harry that's related to them. This is not the time for pride. Remember that long lost cousin with the creaky porch you slept on as a child 40 years ago? Well, they would love to hear from you now, just don't tell them you're down on your luck. If you do they'll just say, "Sorry, wrong number." And, of course, quite a few folks make a beeline straight to the nearest pub. "Bartender, give me a boilermaker. On second thoughts, make that three," or "Bartender, give me a gin and tonic. Hold the tonic."

As luck would have it, yours truly has a lot of experience with homelessness. I've been homeless in Rhode Island, Nashville, L.A., NY, Montana, Seattle, and temporarily in several other places. If you are facing homelessness, or if you already have a berth in the local park, this book is for you. Even if you're not experiencing these disasters you may still learn something from this bittersweet tome. Yes, I do have a comedic approach to this serious topic, but that's by choice. Being homeless is one of the worst afflictions known to man, but if I can cheer myself and others up while discussing this awful event, then I think I've done my job to alleviate the inevitable pain of being non-domiciled. It's a tough, bitter, unforgiving world out there. Someone has to make it tolerable.

Throughout this book, I use phrases like "my street brothers and sisters" or "sistren and brethren", "ladies and germs", "boys and girls", and so on. Prior to even writing this guide, I hadn't given much thought about gender-neutrality language because my mind was really focused on surviving out here in the concrete jungle, the priority being given to finding places to sleep and food to eat. As the book progressed, and I walked around interviewing people and reading more articles on the internet, I began to notice genderless language slowly creeping into popularity. With that in mind, and I mean no insult to anyone, when I use phrases like "brothers and sisters" I am including all the other genders that exist.

CHAPTER 1
The Zen *of* Elimination

"We have come dangerously close to accepting the homeless situation as a problem that we just can't solve." Linda Lingle, Governor of Hawaii, 2002-2010.

Yuck. I apologize for beginning this book with the dirty stuff, but if it wasn't one of the most pressing businesses of the homeless, I wouldn't have given it such a prominent position. Proper places for elimination is a hot button topic these days, anyway, what with pooping rights being denied to transgender folk in a few of the southern states. More and more, we're seeing a world where gender differences don't, well, make any difference. There's a public park just north of Seattle in Snohomish County that removed the gender signs off their bathrooms' walls. Men and women can use any stall they like, just as long as they lock the door behind themselves and didn't eat a whole can of black beans just a few hours before entering the stall.

For the homeless, the gas stations can be your best friends. If you walk into one to borrow the bathroom key, but you just happen to smell like a landfill exploded in your mouth, then forget about Chevron. The attendant will just look you in your scruffy, dumpster-diving face and say the bathroom is out of order and closed for repairs. And if you ask the attendant where does he go to relieve himself he'll just lie to your face and say he went before he came to work. Hold his number's one and two for eight hours straight? Yep. If you look closely you'll see his nose growing in centimeter increments. Who does he think he's fooling? "Hey," you shout, "I was born in the day, just not yesterday."

Some gas station bathrooms aren't fit for human consumption anyway. How poop always ends up on the seat or wall or ceiling is a mystery, but there it is in all its stomach-churning glory. Who uses these bathrooms? Epileptic blind people with colostomy bags for shirts? It's sometimes just better to take a leak in the bushes than risk your health in one of those devilish restrooms. And some of them, when you turn the water on, that's if they have a faucet in the first place, rusty liquid the color of charcoal drips out. Are you supposed to drink that or bottle it to be tested in a lab for contaminants? And why is it so difficult to find tissue paper in a gas station bathroom? You always end up having to dry your hands on your pants because the blower on the wall doesn't work either.

When you're homeless, and you are relegated to using bathrooms like these, you quickly learn to master the Zen art of the hunched-over poop, like it was an ancient Chinese secret. You just need to take a slightly wide stance over the bowl, steel your back, and go to work. It's not as tough as it seems. Baboons do it all the time; I've seen the nature shows. Of course, they think your living room and kitchen are toilets for monkeys, but that's another issue.

Libraries are a good place to relieve yourself; not in the stacks of course. I mean the bathrooms. They're usually well maintained, and some of them, like the bathrooms in supermarkets or fast food joints, even have their cleaning schedules posted on the door for your convenience. They're also a good place to catch up on your reading, too. Just don't sit in the stall with "War & Peace", though. The librarian will frown on your excessive use and think you're just in there shooting drugs. It's wonderful that you're giving Tolstoy a good look-see but a simple magazine article will do just fine. Of course, libraries aren't open 24 hours a day so you do have to plan accordingly. Some are big, some are small. Some are quiet, and some make an elementary school's playground look like a cemetery.

Controlling your kid isn't that hard, is it? I can feel a stroke coming on the second one starts wailing for his mommy. Yesterday, this kid was screaming so loud I thought the top of my head was going to pop off. I don't know. Maybe it's just me, but wouldn't the ball pit in McDonald's suit them better than a library? Isn't there a Chuck E. Cheese, like, within a 50-mile radius of here? It's a good thing the Good Lord invented heavy metal; anything to tune this circus out.

Some supermarkets are open around the clock. That's not necessarily good news, though, because a lot of them close from 11PM to 6PM for restroom "maintenance". In other words, find another stall somewhere. This one's "out of order". The sad thing about that inconvenience, by the way, is that it was forced upon the homeless by the homeless. Supermarket managers don't have a choice in doing that because some homeless folks will shoot drugs in the bathrooms at night or throw their poop on the ceilings and walls for fun. Who wants to scrape turd off a ceiling in the middle of the night? For the restrooms that are open, just show the proprietors a little respect and clean up after yourself. No one's ever died wiping off a toilet seat, as far as I know anyway. Just don't do what some people do – unroll all the toilet tissue and drop it on the floor for fun. That's just ridiculous, yet I see it all the time.

If you're lucky you may find a department store that's open all hours of the night. Wal-marts usually are. The one here in Seattle is a pain in the neck to get to, though, because it's so far out of town, and that's because there's a city-wide effort to keep the 'mom and pop' vibe going strong around here. Of course, with 65 new buildings being built downtown right town, the Walmartization of the Emerald City is a moot point. At least Wal-Mart allows RV's and cars to camp out in their parking lot, too.

Personally, I think that's pretty good customer service. If you wearily get out of your camper to use their bathroom at 2AM, chances are you'll stop and buy something like coffee or a crumb cake. Plus, you are always free to stop and talk to the overnight stockers. They can get pretty bored talking about the same female country music star day in and day out so a little diversion is more than welcome.

In a city like Seattle which is permanently under construction, Porta Johns and Honey Buckets can be found almost everywhere. Feel free to utilize them. They're never locked. Construction guys tend to be relatively clean and respectful of those kiosks so you don't have to worry about poop falling off the ceiling while you're taking a crap.

Did you ever see the indie movie "Trainspotting"? There was a scene where this guy dived head first and swam around in the "worst toilet in Scotland." It's a good thing they didn't say "the world" because the worst toilet I've ever had the pleasure of encountering was the latrine at Arcadia Park in Rhode Island. Talk about filthy! It made the "worst toilet in Scotland" look like Martha Stewart's bedroom. Not one square inch of the latrine was free of poop. There was even poop on the one incandescent bulb dangling precariously off the shit-plastered ceiling. The toilet was absolutely unusable. There was no clean place to stand, and obviously, squatting down was a no-no. And it's too bad, though, because just the name of the park, Arcadia, makes the place sound like a paradise. You really can't judge a book by its cover.

Seattle has a pilot program for the homeless called "Safe Parking". You sign up with them during the day, and at night, you can park your car in the lot of a designated church. You are free to use the restrooms in the house of worship and, if you're lucky, they might even have coffee and donuts for your dining pleasure. A lot of churches also host AA and NA meetings. Even if you're not an addict you can still sit in the sessions, they won't mind. Plus, they all have caffeine and Kaiser rolls so one can't complain.

The alternative to using a public restroom is –ta-daa! - not to use one at all. Yeah, that's impossible, so what you can always do is lessen the number of trips you have to make to the head. To accomplish this, you'd have to drastically change your diet. I knew this old woman in a nursing home who hated eating rice because she had to use a wooden spoon to remove her waste. In other words, give Uncle Ben's a try. If you're like the old woman, you should be able to go for days without hitting the loo.

Apples work just as well, too. For two days, I made the mistake of eating nothing but red delicious. When I finally went to the bathroom on the third day, it was like trying to push a basketball out of my bowels. I'm sure the people standing outside could hear me grunting with my forehead pressed up against the door. When I exited that room, I must've looked like Hot Stuff, the Little Devil. But, that's life. You gotta take the good with the bad. It's probably also better not to eat just soup. You'll be on the can so many times during the day the clerks at Chevron will start thinking you're partying in there. Just keep lots of fiber in your system because you've got better things to do than give your intestines a workout every hour or so.

CHAPTER 2
I'm Gonna Wash That Leaf Right Out *of* My Hair

"We just can't stop people from being homeless if that's their choice." Tony Abbott, Prime Minister of Australia, 2013-2015.

No one wants to smell like a hog-nosed skunk decomposing on a Sub-Saharan desert; definitely not a good way to win friends and influence people, I can assure you. It's bad enough being homeless and separated from the "normal" world; now, being isolated from your street brothers is just adding insult to injury. This is where your creativity, or unconventional thinking, comes in handy. First, you can't be scared of water. It won't melt you like a witch from Oz. If you can drink it, you can bathe in it. Secondly, it's much easier to come by than you'd think. Allow me to count the ways.

Public Showers. Here in Seattle you can find showers at any one of the three Urban Rest Stops - one in Ballard, one downtown and the other in the U-district. Naturally, they're all free to use and they do provide you with a towel if you wish. They're open for usage during daylight hours and their locations can be gleamed from the internet. Other cities have services similar to the three Stops but their names will be different, some being attached to ministries and so on. The Compass Center in Pioneer Square, downtown Seattle also has a bunch of free showers to use. They have a strict 15-minute policy. Stay in the shower any longer than that and they'll assume you've went from scrubbing your arms to shooting in them, so chop chop.

Green Lake also has public showers and they're open six days a week, from 10AM to 8PM and on Saturday, 9AM to 8PM. It's closed on Sundays. I memorized their hours because those are the only showers I use. Towels cost just 50¢ but you do have to return them. The water there is nice, warm and soothing. The only caveat is, to save water, you can't let the it run; you have to hold the shower switch in. Minor inconvenience but still worth its free cost. Feel free to bring your own soap but they do have liquid Dial in wall-mounted dispensers you can use. BTW, if you're shy about other people seeing you in the buff, skip Green Lake. Really, though, you shouldn't be afraid of showering publicly. No one will laugh or say anything to you. Everyone minds their own business. Just look out for the guys who should've been done showering five minutes ago but are still under the water. Obviously, they're looking for more than that last speck of dirt under their fingernails.

Truck Stops. The last time I used the shower at one of these was in the summer of 2006 in Nashville, TN. It cost $7.00 back then but I see now from scanning the internet than they can cost upwards of $12. That price would be too expensive for the average pauper but at least you are guaranteed privacy and a clean towel to boot. Truck stops used to get a bad rap, and to a certain extent, still do because a lot of folks see them as sordid places where Mikey and John Boy can get in a minute or two of hanky-panky before continuing on their long haul runs to Arizona and Kentucky. If that's your thing, more power to you. Ain't no judges here at Planet Robin. Just bring protection and clean up after yourself. No one wants to slip and fall because of some slimy goo beneath their bare feet. Also, keep a sharp lookout at all times to your surroundings. Drugs are bought and sold there and they're sometimes good hiding places for escaped convicts and other criminals, so you never know.

YMCA's. Good place for a nice warm shower; too bad they're not free to use. The showers, saunas and pools are free if you've paid for a monthly or yearly pass; otherwise it'll run you $4 to $6 a pop to shower. Like truck stops, YMCA's are also a good place to mingle. I'm not saying that because I cruised there. I didn't. I'm just going by the Village People song. If they say, *"They have everything for you men to enjoy, you can hang out with all the boys…"* who am I to argue? Naturally, when I say YMCA I also mean YWCA because the same things occur in those places, too. If I was talking about anyone but the homeless, this is the part I'd mention health spas, power yoga shops, 24hr fitness centers and all those hoity toity places where you can get your nails done while sipping your Chai Crème Frappuccino in a comfy leather chair. Since I'm not, get thee to a YMCA, young man, otherwise, check out Number 4 coming right up.

Water Sprinklers. Okay, this is ghetto, and yes, I've done it a few times. Franklin, Tennessee is a fairly quiet, sunny suburb just south of Nashville with lots of condos, cute subdivisions, wide boulevards, beautiful hotels, restaurants, malls and shopping centers galore. And sprinklers. Lots of them. Around 4AM some of those sprinklers automatically come on in different places – an office center here, a furniture shop there, etc. If you're a master of the one minute shower, there's no reason why you can't quickly strip naked in the relative dark of the watered lawn, jump into the water, and sponge yourself off before the police come and drag you off to central booking. Since the water is going to be cold you may as well make the shower as quick as possible. You know, if I do happen to get careless one day and get caught doing that, I'll plead ignorance. "Officer," I'd explain, "I don't see any signs banning nude showers in public sprinklers." I have a feeling he'd let me off the hook just for being as dumb as a box of bricks, but if I did get arrested just for that, that'll be some story to tell the grandkids, huh?

Fountains & Hydrants. Again, ghetto. You see this a lot in the inner cities – busted hydrants with their watery guts spewing out at 30 MPH onto the hot concrete amidst the tenements. It's a free and fun way to cool down – for kids. If you're an adult, not so much. People will probably frown on you if you try it; that doesn't stop adults from enjoying the bath, though. A few precincts in certain jurisdictions have days when they turn the hydrants on themselves to keep an otherwise explosive neighborhood from going up in flames. It's a strategy that seems to work – the police are happy, the people are happy, everyone's happy. Most fountains are smaller than the water spout from a hydrant, unless you happen upon the great fountain in Seattle Center. Again, the sprayed water there is for kids only and adults will get a vicious scouring if they dare jump in the water. I've seen a few grownups do it, though, and no one said anything. Maybe I'm just too old school. Knock yourself out. Go jump in the fountain; just don't say that Robin sent you.

Swimming Pools. No, I'm not talking about Little Johnny's three-foot long Sponge Bob Square Pants' junior pool and spa. I'm talking about the giant Olympic-sized ones that are available during the summer in certain parks nationwide. To get into some of those pools you have to prove you work or live in the same neighborhood as the pool, or pay for a seasonal permit, or pay a small entry fee or, if you get lucky, go swimming for free. Prices change based on whether anyone drowned in the pool the year before and now the city's insurance premium is so high that they have no choice but to charge higher prices. I'm joking, of course. (That's what clowns do). It's best to just check a local library and see what's available in the area you just happened to drift into that day. If all the pools cost too much, there's always…

The Rain. Don't laugh. It can be done. Rain is not just for setting a romantic mood in superhero films or Jennifer Aniston comedies. The sound of that cascading stream is relaxing and could lull any baby into a coma. Unfortunately, runoff from a building can be pretty cold and forceful – an urban waterfall, if you will. Yes, I've bathed in them, but only for a short time because the water's so damn frigid it makes your nards fly up into your chest for warmth, then you have to end up spending the rest of the week trying to get those hairy twins back where they belong. Very annoying.

The Beach. Well, it is water, and it is wet, but that doesn't necessarily translate into getting clean. I've tried the beach-only way and it really doesn't work. When you dry, you can still feel the grit from the ocean on your skin. The beach is perfect, though, if you'd just drunkenly gutted a deer and you covered yourself from head to toe with blood. Lesson for today: don't gut a deer while you're drunk unless you have a beach nearby.

The Art of the One Minute Shower. I hold a black belt in this, achieved when I spent an entire summer in sweltering Nashville, the music capital of America. Like a lot of hopefuls, I drove to Music City with my guitar and thought I'd be able to write songs for Kenny Chesney and Martina McBride. I did make a few contacts but, in the end, it didn't pan out and I eventually succumbed to the loneliness and disappointment of the attempt. I did, however, perfect the craft of showering quickly. In all honesty, it's not really a shower; more like a quick, rejuvenating session. First, you go into a bathroom, any bathroom, and quickly remove your clothes. (It's better if you've already loosened up your belt, shoe laces and other items before going into the public bathroom to help facilitate your speedy execution). Grab a lot of paper towels, get them nice and wet, add a little soap from their dispenser, and quickly wipe your body down. Take some new paper towels, soak them quickly, and wash the soap off your body. Now, with lightning speed, take a handful of paper towels and dry up your mess. You don't want to leave any footprints. Proprietors frown on you using the bathroom as, well, a bathroom, so the drier you make the place the better. Now, you quickly don your clothes and walk out calmly as if all you did in there was piddle.

I used to do the one minute shower business in gas station bathrooms, Wal-Mart, the bathrooms in fast food joints like Mrs. Winner's, and any other place where you had the room to yourself for a short while. Obviously, you're inviting trouble if you did this where other people will see you and notify management. I tried washing myself in the bathroom of a park one day. Smack in the middle of my scrub down, a man came in to use the bathroom. Instead of taking a leak he turned and walked out. Naturally, my spider senses went haywire and I hurried to finish up. Mere seconds later, sure enough, a park ranger entered and said I am forbidden to wash my body in public like that. "Okay," I said as I put on the rest of my clothes. "Won't happen again." Technically, he could've banned me from the park altogether but I am grateful that he didn't. The park also doubled as my bedroom and it would've hurt to burn that bridge.

CHAPTER 3
To Eat *or* Not *to* Eat, That *is* The Question

"The world of the homeless is a tough and interesting world."
Paul Dano, actor.

Wouldn't it be nice that, once people become homeless, they turn into olms? Olms are underwater salamanders from Italy that can go 10 years without eating. That means you can skip the various food pantries, food banks and churches that serve hot meals and spend your days walking to every city and town in the Continental U.S., or finally getting around to writing a book that rivals "War & Peace" in length. Seriously, though, hunger is one of the most important unfortunate circumstances all homeless people face. The food stamps some receive aren't enough, unless they only eat, say, potatoes every day. A 20-pound box of Russet potatoes costs around $15, so if you buy 200 pounds of potatoes/month, you'd spend $150 plus shipping costs. That's not bad actually, but as they say, man cannot live on Russet potatoes alone. So where is a poor homeless bloke supposed to find food for free where he can eat nutritionally and not have to worry about vultures circling in the sky up above where he rests every day?

Food Banks. I have yet to encounter a neighborhood bereft of a food bank, a place where you stand in line (without pushing or shoving like pigeons do), show them your picture ID (a driver license or Dept. of Corrections ID will do), then pick out your allotted amount of vittles for the next few days. Some food banks have better selections that others, so if you're the picky type, you can travel around from bank to bank to see which suits you best. There is a catch, though. Some banks will only serve to people who live in a particular zip code so it behooves you to research where you can shop outside your jurisdiction.

Generally, food banks serve two types of customers – "cooks" and "no cooks". The "cooks" get a chance to pick up refrigerated and frozen products like eggs, milk, cheese and meats as well as dry goods like pasta, potatoes and rice. The homeless-in-the-street populace gets a much smaller selection usually consisting of crackers, tuna, peanut butter, canned peas and beans, pastries, tossed salads, corn chips and the like. It's not bad really, but it is fascinating, or should I say ridiculous, to hear customers in the banks yelling at the volunteers because they don't like the selections. You always hear someone complaining about the color of the bananas, the stiff, generic hot dogs or the fact that the milk available is 2% and not whole. Anyway, there's always Amazon if people aren't pleased. They deliver. Or better yet, they can go get a job at Four Seasons. You can eat all the Wagyu Beef Culotte or Fennel Crusted Halibut you want; at least the leftovers, anyway.

You can still be homeless and get the dried goods like rice and pasta if, like me, you have a hot pot. I bought a used one for $8 from Goodwill. It worked well for a while but I pushed it too hard and burned out its fuse. I have yet to replace it as of this writing. It's a pretty nice appliance, too – a Wolfgang Puck mini rice cooker. The one I have is lime green; that's okay, but because I plug it in downtown amidst the black benches and light poles, you can see it from a mile away. I'd prefer not to draw attention to myself; then again, the Puck cooks so quickly it's not like I'm sitting there stirring the food for hours.

There's a world of difference between eating ravioli cold right out of the can and heating it up. Both will fulfill their intended purpose but the heated version catapults you back into civilization. Finding a place to plug in, unfortunately, can be a real pain in the tookus. So far, in all the parks I've visited in Seattle, not one of the power outlets sitting in the shelters work. Either they're that way to discourage camping or it's just my luck that they'll all non-functional.

The restrooms don't have outlets, either, so that's a wash out. Technically, there is power – just adapt the overhead lights into some type of ghetto power strip, but I'm quite sure the park rangers would frown upon your creativity.

Churches. You can kill two birds with one stone at a church, eat and get religion, both at the same time if you want. All the social service agencies in a particular jurisdiction keep lists of the churches that serve hot meals as well as toiletries, clothing and, if you're lucky, bus passes. I've been to a few of these churches, not just in Seattle but in other cities like L.A., Nashville, Providence, NYC and upstate NY. Most of them don't require you to sit through a service before you eat, but some do.

If you're not a religious person, then sitting through a service can be like getting your toenails pulled out with pliers. Here, patience is a virtue; may as well sit through it because it may be your one chance to eat for the rest of the day. Our Redeemer Lutheran Church here in Seattle doesn't serve hot meals every day, but they do serve Thanksgiving dinner where, at that time, you can also get a ticket for a sleeping bag. That's where I got the comfy one I use now.

Restaurants. This is rare, but from time to time, local restaurants do serve free meals. You usually find out the date and time from food banks. This usually occurs mostly during the Christmas holiday, but occasionally, you just have to keep your eyes peeled. A friend of mine once went to a Mexican restaurant and told them he was starving to death. They pitied him and gave him a chicken chimichanga. I suppose begging for food in a restaurant is a bit of a stretch, and quite humbling to boot, but I guess you never know until you try. I haven't had the nerve to do it because I have enough food from the banks.

In my neck of the woods, the hipsters and yuppies aren't so bad; in fact, they come in handy. When they go out to eat in these tony restaurants, they sometimes get their extra food put in a doggie bag which, believe it or not, they leave out in the street for the homeless. It's not as bad as it sounds. At least it's a pleasant diversion from the usual bland fare you get from the churches and banks. I'm lucky in that a lot of the hipsters and yuppies around here are vegan or vegetarian, meaning whatever they leave out in the street often goes untouched by my fellow carnivorous brothers and sisters. At times, they donate food like jackfruit burritos, spinach and tofu quiche, blackened tofu steak with mango sauce, aloo gobi (cauliflower and potatoes sautéed with tomato and spices), quinoa stir fry, kale & arugula salad with pesto vinaigrette, etc. I couldn't afford to buy those dishes anyway. $15 for a vegetable burrito? Sorry, no can do. Eat like a prince, dine like a pauper. That's me in a nutshell.

There are ghetto ways of getting free food from restaurants but I don't advocate those at all (so put away those German cockroaches. There're not needed here). Some eateries give free food away on specific holidays like Veteran's Day, Thanksgiving, your birthday and Christmas Day. Some restaurants give away free food all year round. A quick Google search will reveal who they are. Most, if not all, serve vegetarian and vegan fare, so if you're okay with mushroom risotto, avocado quesadilla, or any other kind of meatless comfort food, then you're in luck.

To tell you the truth, I don't even know what meatless comfort food is; I just threw that in because I found it on the internet. What is comfort food? Is that, like, opposed to non-comfort food? Food that makes you uncomfortable, like beef stroganoff covered in maggots or ice cream with chards of metal in it? Steak so green it moves by itself? Isn't all food supposed to make you comfortable? What am I missing here?

Ethnic Centers. Some cities and towns have community centers that are based on countries of origin – La Raza Latino Centers, African-American Institutes, Native American Centers, Asian-Pacific Islander Clubs and so on. As far as I know, none discriminate based on race; they were simply set up by their individual peoples to serve their people, but all are welcome. They're usually multi-platform centers, meaning some have schools, some have their own food bank, some serve hot meals, etc. Social service organizations like these can be located online, at your local DSHS or libraries everywhere. For your convenience, Chapter 40 has an easy to make dish inspired by these centers. Your friends will love the multiplicity of flavors and beg for more. Feel free to skip ahead to it at your leisure.

CHAPTER 4
To Sleep, Perchance *to* Dream

"We think sometimes that poverty is only being, hungry, naked and homeless. The poverty of being unwanted, unloved and uncared for is the greatest poverty. We must start in our own homes to remedy this kind of poverty." Mother Teresa, Roman Catholic nun and missionary, recipient of the Nobel Peace Prize, 1979.

This is the tricky part – where to rest your weary, thought-filled, probably inebriated head at night. *[This section doesn't cover shelters. Those are saved for their own section because they are a special world unto themselves].*

If you're a falling down drunk, then the answer is easy: pick a bench. Any bench. Or park. Or beach. Or bridge. Not all benches will work, of course. Some of them have a protruding divider right in the middle of the seat which makes it impossible for any normal being to get some shut eye. If, however, you happen to be one of those Ukrainian contortionists that accidentally missed the last bus back to the airport, then these types of benches would suit you just fine. Parks are a mixed bag. Some cities will let you sleep in them overnight. In Seattle, the parks are off limits from 11:30PM to 4AM. Of course, that doesn't stop people from camping there at those times, and truth be told, the police don't bother to kick you out if you're well behaved and not shooting into the veins in your ankles, otherwise it's well within their rights as enforcers of the law to drag you out to the sidewalk by your hamstrings.

Beaches are cool places to chill while your Malibu condo's getting the new roof put in. Since a bit of the shoreline has eroded here in Seattle and other cities along the Pacific coast, some of the beaches are as rocky as Ben Grimm's face. They're not soft, windswept, or sexy, even if there's a full moon out. Still, I suppose it's better than nothing. Just beware of beaches like the ones in Far Rockaway. I've seen them. They're full of needles. Some of them also have gallons of oil that was deposited there from a tanker's accidental spill half a mile at sea. If you're lucky, your beach may even have a boardwalk. Be careful setting up your blanket under them, though. Those little black logs you're seeing ain't ocean driftwood.

Would you find it impossible to sleep below a bridge with traffic carrying on overhead day and night? A lot of folks don't. To them, that familiar sound of tires on concrete is like a babbling brook to a baby. Most cities don't like people camping out beneath bridges, though. They consider it an eyesore and claim it's dangerous. Hell, going to the mall or the airport on any given day is dangerous. A bridge is probably safer by comparison. In any case, if the police happen to stop by and rouse you awake, they'll just move along eventually since there aren't too many open beds in the shelters anyway.

Hammocks are relatively cheap. I used to have one that cost about $3. Yes, it was pretty cheap, but for all intents and purposes, it worked. Real easy to carry around, too, since it's compact and light. I used to string mine between two trees out in the woods; took me an average of 1 ½ minutes to do it, too. If you have the stones, you can sling a hammock between trees that sit just off any unrestricted suburban road and rest there. It's risky but at least you won't have any furry critters crawling over you at night looking for dinner. Would I string up my hammock in a city park that says "Closed between 11:30PM to 4AM"? Sure, I would. If the police wake me, they wake me. No harm done. I'll just grab my things and move along till I find something else, like another park or a narrow alley between two buildings. If you'll notice, I talk about trees, birds, parks, hammocks and other things with a nature angle to them. That's because I don't even bother with sleeping down in the congested city areas. They're too noisy, dirty, smelly and dangerous. People in those areas are constantly fighting. The screechy noise from the incessant sirens of the fire trucks, squad cars and ambulances could drive you nuts. I'd rather take my chances in a park. Less turmoil for me, anyway.

The U.S. has miles and miles of railroad, and all railroads have a depot. Some depots are so large that sections of it hardly ever see any foot traffic. Those isolated corners are perfect for getting a little shuteye. They're also choice places for drug users to go, so you really have to be careful that you're not usurping someone else's spot. They kinda frown on trespassers. The BNSF line that flows through the Pacific Northwest contains depots which contain lots of empty, albeit rusty, shipping containers. Most of the train yards are locked, but since you're homeless, they're not locked to you. Well, they are, but just tell the authorities you can't read so you didn't know that big white sign on the fence with the red letters said "No Trespassing". These companies have started getting clever, though. Gone are the days of barbed wire fences. The fences I saw recently have these long, sharp, electrified spikes sticking out of them that look like they could circumcise a horse. If the depot you discovered has those inhuman things, then it's time to mosey on along. Why stick around where you're not wanted, right?

Marinas are a good place to get some sleep, too. Not the marinas or the boats directly, but the buildings near the docks. The businesses there – boat suppliers and fitters, yacht sellers, repair facilities, catamaran insurance agents, and so on, are closed at night, making the back of their shops good places to take a load off. Again, like anywhere else, don't get mad and throw a fit if Port Authority comes by, shines a flashlight in your eyes, and tells you to skedaddle. They're just doing his job. All it means is it's time to just pack your things and move on.

If you just so happen to wander near an airplane-construction yard, and you can't read the huge signs everywhere that says 'Trespassers Will Be Shot', feel free to sneak into the yard and try the doors of some of those decommissioned aircraft. You may get lucky and find one or two of them are open. Quickly climb in, quietly shut the door behind you, set up the sleeping bag you got from the Lutheran Church last Thanksgiving, and try to imagine Pictures of Lily while you're drifting off into the netherworld. By the time the foreman discovers you, the sun would be up and all he'll say is, "You Can't Sleep Here," but you already knew that.

When I worked in Wal-Mart in Franklin, TN, the manager let me sleep in my car in the huge, well-lit parking lot. Later, I found out he wasn't really doing me a favor at all – Wal-Mart already had a policy in place where anyone could camp overnight in their parking lot in either a car or RV. Too bad other retail centers aren't so generous.

Just try the same feat at Target's or Sear's and you could count the minutes tell a Security Guard comes along and tells you to take off. Anyway, that's one of those times when it's better to not have a car since a lot of these giant businesses are surrounded by thick maple and elm groves which are perfect for concealing the sleeping human body at night. Don't tell them Robin sent you, though. They're getting tired of hearing my name being called as an excuse for trespassing.

Ella Fitzgerald, Queen of Jazz, use to sleep on the rooftops of buildings in Harlem when she was a teenager. Shania Twain used to sleep in buses. Jim Carrey and his family lived in a car. Practically anywhere there is no security prodding around at night is an okay place to sleep. I, myself, wouldn't sleep in a bus or train station. Too much riff raff running around trying to cause trouble. The old Seattle Times building was once occupied by the homeless but they got kicked out. As a matter of fact, they've been kicked out about three times, maybe more. Usually they just stay gone for a day or two then slowly move back in after the police went looking elsewhere for bigger fish to fry. There was a guy who once stowed away on the landing gear of a jet airliner. When the plane landed, they found him. The authorities were surprised he didn't freeze to death considering how cold it can get at 30,000 feet. I don't know if he slept the whole time he was in the gear, but it's not something I recommend. You're just trying to get a little shut, not turn into Wesley Snipes in *"Demolition Man"*.

CHAPTER 5
Don't Let *the* Bastards Grind You Down

"Let me give up attachment through unattachment. My soul will be my only support (in this practice of unattachment). (Hence) let me give up everything else." Mahavira. 24th Tirthankar of the Jain Dharma.

I heard from a reliable source that the police department frowns upon homeless people who carry guns. I don't know if that's true or not but I'm not gonna tempt fate by arming myself with a 9mm. I know a couple of folks who keep weapons like knives and baseball bats and, like the American Express Card, they'll never leave home without them. I'm lucky in that I'm nearly six feet tall, a male and kinda look ½ crazy. I also speak with a Trinidadian accent which some people mistake for Jamaican. This comes in handy because, for some reason, people view Jamaicans as being as vicious as nurse sharks. I'm not complaining. Hey, if that's what it takes to keep me safe, pass the dutchie to the left-hand side. Is that seen?

Knives. These come in all shapes and sizes, from the janbiyas (the curved daggers all Yemeni men wear to scare suitors away from their female relatives) to the *kila* (a three-sided knife used in Tibet to exorcise demons out of the devilishly afflicted). If, however, you have no young female relatives and no one you know is spitting out split pea soup in massive quantities, then a simple folding pocket knife should suffice. These are perfectly legal to keep on your person as long as the blades are 4 inches or shorter. In some states, 2 ½ inches is the most so you'd have to check local laws. In Texas, it's 7", but that's Texas. Everything's gotta be larger than life. You also should try your best not to walk around with your blade in plain sight. Here's why:

A few years ago, near-deaf Native American woodcarver John T. Williams of Seattle was strolling down the street (Boren, I believe) with his carving knife and a wooden board the size of a phone book. A cop noticed this, leaped out of his car, and ordered John to drop the blade. Poor John didn't hear the officer and was consequently shot four times to death within four seconds of being told to drop the knife. Naturally, there was a big uproar amongst the Native American community and they protested. The officer, Ian Birk, resigned from the SPD. No one knows where he is now. My money's on Hayden Lake, Idaho in the cabin right next to Mark Furhman's trailer. The city gave John's family $1.5 million bucks and told them to try and put this tragedy behind them. I've always believed that the cop shot the wrong person, that is, had it been a black man, Seattle would've gone up in flames. That's in stone. Lesson learned: it's okay to keep a knife for protection, just be careful about walking with it out in the open in public.

Pepper spray. I hate those things. One particularly chilly night, with nothing on TV but reruns of "Bewitched" and a handful of shopping channels, I decided to go on an ill-advised drug run. Chill or no chill, the dealers were still going to be out. There could've been 10 feet of snow but you can bet they would be out there like Buddy Rich, never missing a beat. By the time I arrived at the dog park on 3rd Avenue, I started sobering up. The white-robed conscience on my right shoulder whispered in my ear to forget my run and just go home; the red-robed devil on my left said, "Eh, you already went through all the trouble driving down here, plus, its 1AM. You know it'll be a few hours till you start getting sleepy." So, flicking the angel off my right shoulder, I carried on with my late-night quest.

I ran into a cliché on 2nd Avenue – a black man with a white girl. You can spot who's carrying from afar because they're usually ambulatory, the girl being the mule and the black guy who determines if it's okay to sell stuff to strangers. After I picked up a 20, I quickly walked back to my car parked just a few blocks away. As I was getting in it, a clean cut, fairly good looking guy in his late 20's approached and asked me if I could break him off a piece. I shook my head and lied, "I got nothing." He quietly said, "Okay," then casually whipped out a container of pepper spray, squirted its fiery content into my left eye, then turned and ran while I squirmed like a salted slug. I didn't scream out or anything, but it sure hurt like hell. So now, being in way too much pain to go after him on foot, I simply chalked it up as a learning experience and drove home with my tail between my legs.

I was saved permanent damage to my left eye because I wear contacts. Good thing, otherwise I would've had to wear an eye patch and spend the rest of my life getting used to being called Slick Rick or Nick Fury. So, yes, pepper spray can be a valuable deterrent to tote around. They're relatively cheap (about $10), compact, and can usually be attached to your key chain. Dick's Sporting Goods, Wal-Mart and Amazon carry quite a few, so choose wisely. They come in three strengths, Levels I – II – III. Level I will shoo Mrs. Birdsong's yippy, annoying little Chihuahua away from your heels. Level II should slow her German Rottweiler down should it get loose from the Kevlar-reinforced cage she keeps it in. Level III will make a Columbian black bear think twice about raiding your campsite as well make a crackhead crap his pants as he's running away from you with lava-like tears in his burning eyes. Level III, you see, is loaded with more capsaicinoids (chemicals found in chili peppers) than the other two and is the preferred strength of the NYC police. You can also use mace if no pepper spray is available. Mace is a tear gas, and as such, should slow an attacker down…unless they're under the influence of drugs or alcohol where it has absolutely no effect. Seeing that the people trying to rob you are looking for money for drugs as opposed to sending their daughters through college, stick with the pepper spray. It'll bring them to their knees faster than a priest in a boy's club.

Stun guns. The price on these came down significantly in the past 10 years or so. You can buy one now, with a built-in 120dB alarm and LED flashlight, for about the same amount of money you'd pay for a stuffed spinach & broccoli pizza from Sbarro's, about $22. Stun guns will straighten the pubes out of anyone who attacks you, but they have to be within close range. You lay one of these 60,000,000 volt puppies on a bad guy then stand back as he drops to his knees since you just forced his brain to stop sending signals to his voluntary muscles. Pretty eerie, but it works…most of the time. Yep, just like mace, some people are so tweaked out that no amount of voltage will slow them down, making you resort to plan B – the Mac-

10 you keep in your right pants leg. Tasers are similar to stun guns in that tasers emit electrodes which attach to an assailant up to 15 feet away and the effect is pretty much the same. Since they're regulated the same as firearms, you really only see them being used by law enforcement. It's said that Rodney King was hit twice with tasers but he didn't drop because he was hopped up on PCP. If that's true, and I don't know if it is, then tasers may not always be the best tool for the job.

Personal alarms. These work well if you're being dragged into a dark alley by two meth heads in downtown Atlanta but they're worthless if you're being assaulted by Crackhead Casey in an isolated part of Forest Park about ½ mile from the nearest roadway. They are pretty loud, though. 130bB is powerful enough to catch people's attention for blocks but not powerful enough to make your attacker's ears bleed. Still, if your assailant has the spine of a jellyfish, he'll run off. Alarms are pretty compact and cost around $20. Like pepper sprays, they can be attached to your key ring or even dangled in a chain from around your neck. Unlike other self-protection devices, alarms are legal in all 50 states, including airplanes, so you don't need to consult your local jurisdiction about carry rules or keep a copy of the 2nd Amendment folded in your wallet just in case. BTW, if you're thinking about breaking into somebody's back yard to steal some of their prized Bietigheimer apples from a tree, don't attempt it if they have a pair of St. Bernard's from Cujo's bloodline and all you're just armed with is a 130dB alarm. Not only will you just annoy the massive dogs, they will tear you limb from limb when all they would have probably done is lick the sweat off your face.

Martial arts. Can you kick like Jet Li? How about punch like Muhammad Ali? If you can't run like Usain Bolt, then maybe it's time to beef up those spaghetti arms of yours and learn a little kung fu before sleeping in that cheap polyester hammock at the edge of Needle Park especially since it contains more cigarette burns than the four thousand holes in Blackburn, Lancashire.

There are many ways to hone up on your fighting skills, from library books and dojos to Latinx Paco, the Guazabara expert from

Manhattan's Lower East Side. On second thoughts, forget Paco; he spends more time in jail than Charles Manson since he's the bagman for half the base heads in Atlantic City. They say he gets himself busted on purpose because he makes more money as a power bottom for all the rich hetties in Atlantic City Jail, but that remains to be seen. So where is a self-respecting wimp supposed to learn the ancient art of hand to hand?

Private instructors are probably the best way to go unless you're one of these super autistic kids who can learn to fight like Jackie Chan just from studying his moves in the films he makes. If, however, you're not that gifted, then feel free to visit several martial arts training academies in your neck of the woods. They're pretty popular now since Bruce Lee became a legendary figure back in the 70's. Which fighting arts should you learn? There's no right or wrong answer to that question. Think about it. You wouldn't walk into Tony Roma's and ask which restaurant makes the best steak. Obviously, they'll say it's them. There are as many fighting styles these days as there are ways to prepare tofu – Krav Maga from Israel, Jiu-Jitsu from Brazil, Taekwondo from Korea, Muay Thai from Thailand, Wing Chun from China, Aikido from Japan, Gatka from India, and so on. The list is endless. A quick search on the internet or your local phone book will point you in the right direction. Just know there is no quick way to learn how to yank out someone's tongue through their windpipe, if that's what you're after, but a little patience will go a long way.

If you must learn how to disarm a robber or incapacitate a rapist quickly then you might have to pass on the fighting schools. They're in the business of teaching self-defense as well as making money. If they're able to turn you into Kwai Chang Caine in three easy lessons, their school would be out of business so fast they'd have to resort to using their deadly skills to rob people on the street. Since street crime is so prevalent everywhere, police stations, community centers and other institutes often offer free self-defense classes from time to time. They're mainly for women, but who says your girlfriend can't teach you a kick or two? Just think: in eight easy lessons, you can turn Big Bad Bill into Sweet William in less time than it takes to boil an egg. If you have $75 to burn and three hours free in the afternoon, and you're a woman, and you live in the Pacific Northwest, you can take the one-day workshop at Fighting Chance Seattle, an empowerment and awareness workshop for women. Can they turn you into Crouching Tiger, Hidden Dragon in just three hours? Well, I doubt they'll train you how to balance on a tree's branch the width of a pencil, but you should learn enough to make any assailant think twice in continuing what evil he had in mind.

There are many other weapons you can carry of course, but they're illegal in most jurisdictions. Weapons such as collapsible batons, billy clubs, brass knuckles, John Steed's bowler hat or umbrella/sword, blackjacks, baseball bats (legal if you're also carrying a baseball), nunchaks (why bother with those – only Bruce Lee knows how to use them anyway), switchblades, daggers, katanas, fighting stars, or those javelin rope darts you see in a lot of Shaw Brothers kung fu flicks are illegal. Would you believe that if you dress up like Indiana Jones or Catwoman for Halloween, carrying a real leather bull whip is legal? Yep. They cost about $30 on Amazon. I'm not sure why anyone would own a bull whip…unless you're whipping bulls which, in my eyes, are an absolute no-no. Then again, if I was staggering drunk one night and got a little too "friendly" with you, feel free to put me back in place with a lash or two. You won't kill me, but man, I'll definitely feel the burn from those welts for the next week or two.

CHAPTER 6

To Spánge *or* Not *to* Spánge: That *is* the Other Question

"I am a gypsy. I haven't had a home for a long time. Call me a homeless person – I just throw everything in a bag and I'm good to go." Taylor Kinney, actor.

"Spánging" (rhymes with changing) is a portmanteau of "spare" and "change". Spánging, then, would be the act of standing in front of Whole Foods with a cardboard sign that reads, "Help! Stranded On Earth. Need Fuel For My Rocket" or something like that. Begging is as old as prostitution, probably even earlier, but for some reason I've never heard of it being called "spánging" till the Pacific Northwest. Maybe it's a politer way of saying panhandling. In any case, begging, spánging, panhandling or prostrating yourself for help from your fellow man exists, ego be damned. Do I encourage asking strangers for money? Well, I have mixed feelings about that.

For: I'm altruistic to the core. I like giving stuff away like food or money, but not for frivolous reasons, of course. I won't buy you wine or weed but I will buy you a loaf of bread or some milk or a granola bar. Giving, I believe, elevates mankind from his propensity for greed. We are, after all, civilized, but not only that, brothers. In addition, apart from giving being a simple act of kindness and humanity, according to Jain beliefs, it's beneficial for your soul.

Karma binds to the soul and erodes it. The idea, then, is not only to prevent the influx of karma but also remove what has accumulated over the years. The soul is thought of as being natural, transparent and pure, but because it is caught in a cycle of birth, death and rebirth, it cannot transmigrate towards its ultimate state because of the pollutant karma. Karma, that which taints the soul, exists as illustrated by the reality of negativities such as sufferings and pain. The idea, then, is to decrease what causes suffering and pain – greed, ego, hatred, jealousy, anger, and so on. If you covet a man's wife or garden or house or boat then you will have sleepless nights trying your best to keep up with your neighbor, perhaps even harboring thoughts of causing him harm to gain your objectives.

Giving, then, is two-fold in intent – when you give, you eliminate your soul-destroying karma that has accumulated over the years. When you receive, you've done your job in helping your fellow man lessen his karma which, in itself, is a good deed which lessens your karma. Thus, altruism is beneficial to both parties and everyone wins.

Against: Believe it or not, I'm only human, and am therefore eligible to be fallible and weak and imperfect like most of us are. Imagine this scenario: from the minute you punch the clock, your supervisor is riding you like a camel jockey, trying his best to squeeze every last drop of blood from your body to fulfill his needs. He'll talk down to you, threaten you with unemployment, perhaps even prevent you from having the same lunch period as Miss Lucy and, therefore, miss your chance in asking her out on a date. At the end of the exhausting day, you are surprised to see the clock you just punched looks just like your supervisor's face. Oh no, wait; it was just a mirage. On your way home, you decide to stop into Associated Market to get a six pack of Corona to wash the taste of your job out of your mouth. As you tiredly approach the store's entrance, a man sitting outside with a sign that says something about rocket fuel asks you for some change. "No!" you think to yourself. "Get a fucking job!" But you're so angry that you just ignore the beggar and continue into the store, never slowing down to give him that nickel that's been sitting in your pocket all day.

When you're tired, the last thing you want to hear on the street is, "Spare some change?" You think, "How dare these people ask me for my hard-earned money? Don't they know what I just went through to be able to enter this supermarket to get me a little bit of beer? Can't they see the baseball-sized bleeding ulcer in the pit of my stomach or the shiny bald spot on my head that gets larger each frigging day?" "No, I don't have any change!" you yell. No one is immune to anger and fatigue, and the less of it you can muster in the course of a day, the better. I closely watch the faces of the aggravated as they come to the store and I can see their anger, their frustration at being asked for money when all they want is to be left alone. And I can sympathize with them because when I went to stores after work with smoke coming out of my ears, the last thing I wanted to hear was, "Spare some change?"

But I'm different now; I'm a little older and a little wiser, I hope. I believe in spánging and I also believe in respecting shoppers' spaces. Aggressive panhandling is illegal and I have even gone so far as to tell my begging brothers that what they sometimes do borders on aggression. I say be patient. If someone wants to give you money they'll come to you. You don't have to say a word. They know what you're out on the street doing; it's not rocket science contrary to what your cardboard sign may say. Everyone benefits from the giving-taking exchange. It's poor taste to go beyond your own boundaries. A little respect goes a long way.

CHAPTER 7

All *the* World's A Busker's Stage

"I was 21 and homeless – such a broken, lost woman." Lykke Li, singer, songwriter, fashion model.

Busking is an art form. It's the art of entertaining people in the street for food and/or money and can include diversions such as playing a guitar or saxophone, miming, belly dancing, acrobatics or what have you. The better you are, of course, the more money you'll make. Young people sometimes travel around the world and busk, not necessarily to make money, but to gain a life experience. How many people can say they strummed a guitar outside the Champs-Elysees or mimed like Marcel Marceau on a London tube?

No one will ever get rich busking; it is a chance, however, to make a little pocket change for a hot dog with sauerkraut or a Mexican beer. Some cities require you to get a permit to perform in public especially if you intend to set up shop in well-travelled sites like the Space Needle or Pike Place Market in Seattle. Pike Place has 13 locations where musicians can perform for one hour or so. The permit costs $30/year and you get an identity badge just in case the Pike Place Police comes around and unplugs your electric cello's amp.

Speaking of cellos, did you ever see the movie The Soloist? It stars Jamie Foxx as a gifted cellist who, unfortunately, becomes the victim of schizophrenia which causes him to become homeless. And since he doesn't have a cello, he plays a two-stringed violin on the street for a little pocket change. It's an inspirational story that also stars Robert Downey Jr. as a newspaper columnist who tries his best to help Jamie get the assistance he needs. (You can read more about The Soloist in the movie review section of this book). Busking is not an easy choice to make. There is always the chance of being ridiculed, of being robbed of your instrument, of being harassed by the police or not making a penny. Nerves of steel is a requirement for busking; the timid would not be able to survive that kind of public scrutiny or constant exposure to the elements for any length of time.

Busking is not a lower art form; just thought I'd put that out there just in case some people are thumbing their noses up at it. Paul McCartney also busked, not only when he was just starting out, but just a few years ago, to gauge people's amusement. Because Paul wore makeup that made him look like the president of the ZZ Top fan club, no one knew who he was as he sat out there on the streets of London playing his guitar and singing. One passerby noted that, even though this "Paul" could sing and play guitar, he sounded nowhere near as good as the real Paul.

Just for the experience, I once busked on the streets of Providence, R.I. I made no attempt to get money; it was just for fun, just me and my amp and electric guitar. It's a good thing I wasn't looking for money because I made none. Okay, I'm no Hendrix, but gee, I don't think I was that bad. Sometimes, though, you might get lucky with some of the free entertainment out there. I'm not talking about the 70-year-old Asian man on the waterfront with the amplified one-stringed Chinese violin that made a sound like an alley cat trying to pass a fist-sized fur ball through its intestines, unless of course that's the kind of sound you're into. There was a violin player I saw, however, that played like he was a soloist with the Vienna Philharmonic. This was down at Westlake Center, a popular spot for busking. I don't remember what the music he played was but it did sound Hungarian or gypsy-influenced like it was written by Brahms or Liszt. So, if you're looking to make a little pocket change, and you have a bit of talent, feel free to tune up your instrument and hit the road. Motown may not come calling but it'll be a better way to spend your time than, say, drying out in jail after a three-day bender.

CHAPTER 8
The Emperor's New Clothes

"I met this homeless man who had never owned a shirt in his life. He had taken his pants and worn them as a shirt and I thought it was so creative. He was liberated from the conventions of fashion." Julia Stiles, actress.

Since this book is about living a clean, crime free existence out in the street, I won't endorse sneaking into your neighbor's yard in the middle of the night and swiping her damp drawers off her clothes line. That's just wrong, not to mention it'll keep bad karma clinging to your soul. You don't want to have a grand piano falling out of the sky on top of you, do you? I think it would suck to have a grand piano drop on top of me from the sky. If I survived it I'd be a cripple for the rest of my miserable life, walking around all hunched over like Quasimodo, resigning the rest of my days to ringing bells in all the churches around town. Bells are rather loud; it probably would've been better if that grand piano had put me out of my misery altogether. But, I digress.

Thrift stores are a homeless person's best friend besides the soup kitchens and food banks. Where else can you get jeans for $5 or t-shirts for $1? There's no shame in buying second hand. I've done it for years, and as long as you keep the clothes clean, people will think you got them off the rack at Nordstrom's anyway. The thrift stores are cool, too, because they do carry name brands like Abercrombie & Fitch, Polo, North Face, Calvin Klein, Sean John or whatever's hip these days. Some of the clothes have such minor imperfections that no one would notice unless you're being scrutinized in the park by your fellow panhandlers. I wonder what would happen if I walked topless into one of those thrift shops one day and told them my shirt and wallet was stolen while I was sleeping in the park. They'd probably give me a shirt, but with my luck, just for a lie like that, a metal safe would drop on me from out of the sky just as I exited the store. Probably better to just ask the manager for a shirt. Who knows? He might be sympathetic and give me one from the back that they were going to throw away because it was beyond repair.

In many cities and towns there are social service agencies that give out vouchers for clothes, furniture, appliances, and the like. They're usually listed in phone books or places like food banks and shelters. Beyond vouchers, you might find there are churches, food banks and ethnic and religious institutions that give out clothes and toiletries on certain days of the week. I, myself, have been pretty lucky. I was sitting at the food bank one day when someone brought in the shoes I'm wearing now, a pair of size 12 Timberlands. They're in pretty good shape too, albeit slightly used. At least they do fit me well. The shirt I'm wearing was just sitting on the ground in an alley between two restaurants. I picked it up, it was my exact size, and tried it on. Perfect. The pants I'm wearing was also dropped off by someone at the food bank. It's a woman's pants but that doesn't matter. No one can tell unless I schooled them. Besides, we're in a brand-new world. Gender specificity seems to be going the way of the dodo bird anyway. Plus, the pants fit perfectly so I can't complain. My socks were donated by a nearby social service agency and my hat was just sitting on a fire hydrant waiting for me to pick up. Can't complain.

I'm sitting in Safeway right now making this entry. It's just past 9PM and the store is relatively empty save for a few yawning workers and one young, anorexic security guard whose slightly belligerent behavior makes him look like he's protecting Fort Knox from an impending terrorist attack, as opposed to making sure some greasy teen isn't trying to make off with a pack of gum in his baggy jeans. The city is filled with these clever petty thieves who strut around with their baggy pants hanging so low that their asses show. Grandma might be offended by their lack of sartorial elegance. Perverts like me, on the other hand, enjoy their minute show of misguided indiscretion; an advertisement, if you will, for a come on.

Making tonight's journal entry is a little tough, not because Safeway only gives me one hour to write this, but because the heavyset homeless guy sitting near me smells like his colostomy bag just exploded beneath his shirt; now he's as funky as Sly & the Family Stone in their prime. I'm surprised this guy's odor doesn't kill the flowers in here. And you know the clothes he's wearing weren't changed since last Christmas. Can you imagine wearing the same thing every day, day in, day out? I do it but I don't have a choice – I only have one change of clothes. Unfortunately, at six months, your underwear can stand by itself. By 12 months, it can walk circles around a sprinter. It surprises me sometimes how people can't smell their own unbearable brand of personal cologne. I don't think anyone's ever died from taking a shower, but I guess there's a first time for everything. I should get up and tell him he can get his laundry done for free at one of the Urban Rest Stops in town, but I have a feeling he'd rather not be bothered. He probably could use hands-on help washing his clothes, I don't know. This is where one's creativity comes in handy.

Back in the old times, way before Maytag and Westinghouse showed up to save the day, there used to be a little item called a scrubbing board. Tanty, my grandmother, would pore over this wooden, ribbed, knee-high contraption on Saturday mornings, scrubbing our wet clothes till her knuckles bled. We kids weren't immune to that kind of labor, either. No scrubbie, no eatie. It was that simple. People still use the scrubbing board around the world, and perhaps even in the Appalachian backwoods, but you'd be hard pressed to find it in Ikea or any store that carries a microwave oven. I mentioned all that to say that washing your clothes by hand is not a lost art. I still do it to this day, mainly in public sinks in gas stations and parks. The owners don't like me doing it, but I wash so quickly they hardly notice. The hand soap in these public places work just fine for cleaning clothes, too. It's not Ming's Chinese Laundry quality, but it'll do. At least flowers won't drop dead from the funk of your dirty clothes when you walk past them. And soap is easy to come by, too, if you don't have it. Every so often you'll get lucky at a food bank where they hand out toiletries in addition to week old bread. Just save up all those small hotel samples. They'll come in handy someday.

Naturally, drying your clothes is the easy bit. There are fences, benches and branches everywhere you look in a community. Just make sure you don't leave your laundry hanging where another homeless person would find it. Yes, you will kiss it goodbye if you're not careful. Your fellow spánger is your friend; just don't keep your back to him too long because, in the streets, there are only two people you can trust – you and yourself. Beware of the airborne birds, too, especially the gulls and crows. They are your friends and companions when you feed them but they'll irritate you in a heartbeat if they decide to 'bless' your drying clothes during a flyover. What's worse than washing your laundry once is washing them twice, and who's got time for that? It's a good thing the birds aren't the size of pterodactyls. You'll be scrubbing your clothes so often the skin on your fingers would rub off.

CHAPTER 9
Making Friends *or* Going It Alone

"When I was 19 years old, both of my parents died in the same year; my mom of cancer and my dad in a car accident. Through the next two or three years and a series of bad decisions   all my own, I might add – I ended up literally homeless, before that was even a word. I even slept occasionally under a pier on the Gulf Coast." Andy Andrews, author and corporate speaker.

At one of the Seattle public libraries I frequent, there is a community center and park next to it. Since the center has external power outlets I sometimes utilize them with my Wolfgang Puck Mini Rice Cooker. Yesterday, late in the evening after the library had been closed for nearly 30 minutes, I sat near the center cooking some Bird's Eye pasta with cheesy broccoli. Meth Mom and Meth Daughter were sitting nearby just whiling the time away. Meth Boyfriend came over and asked Meth Daughter for the name of the dealer who ripped her off. Meth Daughter said she doesn't know his last name. Meth Boyfriend said he needed his first and last name because he doesn't want to kill the wrong person. Meth Mom said the dealer has a Facebook page; just give her a few minutes and she'll find it. That's when I thought I'd heard enough, unplugged my rice cooker, and hauled ass. If someone was going to get shot maybe it's better if I wasn't a witness.

Which brings me to today's chapter, boys and girls: Making Friends or Going It Alone. There are advantages and disadvantages to both. Life, being the fluid machine that it is, sometimes gives you the choice of both and allows you to slide between the two extremes. How well you survive each depends on your ingenuity, talent, hard work and luck. Friends, I must admit, are a tricky lot. Making friends is easy. Keeping them, though, is difficult once your money's run out.

Advantages of Making Friends: You have someone to watch your back (hopefully) when the going gets rough. You have company to talk to should your loneliness start eating you alive. You have someone whose company you are free to enjoy, from walks in the park to sojourns to the nearest Arboretum, from watching a movie on a laptop to taking a toke from a spliff if that's your thing. You have someone to hold your space in the food bank queue should you find it necessary to use the bathroom at that inopportune moment. You have someone to cuddle with when it gets cold at night. You have someone to cheer you up when you get depressed or offer sympathy when they hear all your sad stories. You know, it's funny, well maybe not so funny, but when people haven't seen me for a few days or weeks or months, and then they finally do, they always have that same look on their face, the one that says, "You're still alive? Well I'll be damned!" Geez, are people putting bets on my health that I don't know about? Maybe my lifestyle scares them, I don't know. I do appreciate the concern, though.

Disadvantages of Making Friends: The homeless are an unpredictable lot. Your new best friend could be a fugitive from the law, wanted in several states for armed robbery, manslaughter and 2nd degree sexual assault of his cousin, or he could just be trying to befriend you only to rip you off later. Your new best friend could be running from a gang that, should they catch up to him, they'll kill him and whoever he's with. Your new best friend could have more personalities than Sybil, and one day you could wake up with a hunting knife sticking out of your chest because one of his personalities told him to do that. And sometimes, actually, a lot of times, your new best friend hangs around with the wrong people that could influence you in a negative way, or your friend himself could introduce you to, or retrigger your, alcohol and drug habits. Happens all the time: good kid from the 'burbs turns into bad kid from the projects. Many lives wasted that way. You really can't be too careful.

Advantages of Going It Alone: You can choose to sleep where ever you want and not have to argue with someone about whether it should be in the woods, park or abandoned Chevy. You don't have to share the little food you have or deal with anyone arguing that you use too much or too little seasoning when you cook beans and rice. You can spend all the time you want in a library without someone pestering you about going to the beach or the mountain or the zoo or the Naked Bike Ride Rally and Brewery Festival. You can listen to Beethoven or Judas Priest all day and not have to put up with the greatest hits of Celine Dion, Drake or Lil Wayne. You don't have to worry about someone trying to influence you to do things you'd rather not do, like ripping off old ladies, mainlining heroin, tagging City Hall, catcalling Asian girls at the mall, or visiting his gangsta friend who keeps six red nose pitbulls and an AK-47 on a center table next to a mountain of coke.

Disadvantages of Going It Alone: Four eyes are better than two. (Four actual eyes, not somebody who wears glasses). You're more vulnerable to attacks, muggings and assaults when you're alone. Your loneliness can eat you alive if you don't have much to do. You stand a chance of going crazier faster because you have no one to bounce your ideas off, and if one of those ideas tells you to start a fire in the men's room at Foot Locker, you may do it without contesting. Should you slip down an embankment and break a leg while trying to reach a branch laden with ripe cherries, you have no one to call 911 or drag you to the nearest ER. If the pizza you just warmed up went down your throat sideways, you have no one to perform the Heimlich maneuver on you. You win two tickets to an amusement park or rock concert from the wrapper of a hamburger you just ate, but you throw it away because you know you won't enjoy yourself going alone. You sit in the park eating the African peanut soup you'd just received from the food bank but you can't enjoy it with all the sights of couples walking around hand in hand before you. You constantly have to take your belongings with you wherever you go, even to the bathroom, because it might be gone by the time you're half way through washing your hands.

CHAPTER 10
Chris McCandless – The Interview *from* Beyond

"What difference does it make to the dead, the orphan, and the homeless, whether the mad destruction is wrought under the name of totalitarianism or the holy name of liberty or democracy?" Mahatma Gandhi, the preeminent leader of the Indian independence movement employing nonviolence and civil disobedience.

The Pacific Northwest of the United States of America has unpredictable weather. During the day, say, around noon, you can easily rip off your shirt and run around half naked in a park without feeling so much as a hint of a chill. You stare up at the pristine blue sky and gaze upon miles and miles of wonderful emptiness – no clouds, no white smoke trails from passing jets, no birds of prey scouting for their next meal, nothing. You can practically hear Lou Reed singing its soundtrack in the background – *"Just a perfect day / Problems all left alone / Weekenders on our own / It's such fun."* The serenity makes you slow down to experience the real world so you find a warm spot in the recently cut grass, lie down with your hands folded behind your neck, close your eyes and thank your lucky stars that ISIS isn't sawing your head off with a dull blade and posting those pictures on the internet.

Then something wakes you up; it's a chill wind from the west. You look skyward and notice the perfect blue has been replaced by ominous grey. The goose bumps up and down your arms remind you to don a shirt, perhaps even get up and be on your way, maybe even step inside somewhere because it looks like rain will come soon.

Such was the evening I found myself wandering listlessly up a boulevard looking for shelter, any shelter – a fast food joint, a department store, a skating rink, anything. Then, crack! The sky finally opened up and the drops of water fell down like tears. I quickly looked around for a bus shelter or an eave somewhere when my eyes fell upon a multi-colored hut across the street with its lights on. Instinctively, I ran towards it, nearly getting hit by a passing car. Plodding through puddles of water, I quickly read the sign just outside the hut, "Madame Ang – Fortune Teller", opened the door and entered.

"Hello?" I asked. "Is anyone here?"

Apart from the two floor-standing lamps on opposite sides of the hut, there were Native American tapestries hung on every wall amidst decorations such as a framed pipe collection, framed feathers of all kind, Native headdresses, dream catchers, bone jewelry and other accoutrements reminiscent of the native way of life from the olden days. Up on a shelf, a small stone bowl with a few sticks of sage incense burned slowly, their intoxicating scent enveloping the room like a baby's soft blanket. As I shook out the water my clothes had collected, a native woman of about 70 entered from the back. Standing about 4'11" tall, she wore an eagle-decorated robe with a headband around her silver hair and simple moccasins on her feet.

"Please," she greeted me, pointing to the small round black table in the middle of the hut, "have a seat."

"Thanks," I said, doing as she wished. I watched as she gently took to her own seat.

"What brings you here tonight, Robin?" she asked.

"How do you know my name?" I asked incredulously.

"I'm an oracle," she answered. "That which cannot be read by all can be ascertained by me."

I squinted. Is she for real? Given the mishmash of colors she wore I thought maybe she was just garden variety schizo.

"Is that your name?" I queried. "Ang?"

"It's short for Angwusnasomtaqa. It means Crow Mother Spirit."

"Crow Mother Spirit. That's different. Are you from Seattle?"

"Montana," she replied. "The Crow Rez."

Looking downward at the table, she stretched forth her hands and wrapped them around the teapot-sized glass ball sitting in its wooden base on the rickety table. Behind her head a soft red glow appeared and, just as quickly, dispersed.

"I must be hallucinating," I thought. "Maybe there's something in that incense."

"You're not hallucinating," she said aloud to my surprise.

"You can read minds?" I asked.

"Sometimes," she answered. "Certainly, not all thoughts wish to reveal themselves."

I gently tapped my fingers on the table and stared at her for a few seconds. By nature, I'm a skeptic, scientific to the bone. If it cannot be substantiated, it doesn't exist. TV and the internet is flooded with charlatans who squeeze money out of hopeful, misguided souls who pay to hear that their dead mother is doing well in the afterlife or their own personal bad luck will soon end.

"Would you like to know your fortune?" she asked.

I thought about what she asked for a second but then decided, shook my head and said, "No." If she was about to fill my head with scenes of false prosperity I didn't want to hear it. You can fool some people some of the time, but when it comes to a skeptic, it's best to save your breath.

"You can speak to the dead through me," she insisted.

"Oh, really?" I asked. "Like to my grandfather or something?"

"Anyone you wish," she answered.

"What does it cost, my soul?" I joked.

"It'll cost you nothing," she promised.

I eyed her suspiciously for a scant few seconds then thought about the book on homelessness I was committed to writing. One of the chapters I'd planned would be about the young man who intrigued me by trying to go it alone in the wilds of Alaska to escape the commerciality of life, Chris McCandless, nicknamed Alex Supertramp. I decided to play along.

"Chris McCandless," I told her. "Can I talk to him?"

"Is that a relative of yours?" she asked.

"No," I answered. "I thought you knew everything,"

"Tell me a little about him," she requested, ignoring my doubtful outburst.

"Well," I responded, trying my best to remember what details I knew about Chris. "He was born in California in the late 60's then his family later moved to Virginia. After college, he hitchhiked all the way to Alaska when he around 24 but then died in the forest up there."

Madame Ang, remaining absolutely silent, closed her eyes and slowly rubbed the glass ball.

I thought about bouncing while her eyes were closed, but it was coming down so hard outside I just decided to play along for a short while till it died down.

"Evening, Robin," Ang said without opening her eyes. Her voice had changed. Before, it sounded old and quivery, almost dissonant, typical of someone about 70; now it sounded younger, more sure, almost as if she were a young woman again. It was also devoid of the native accent she'd spoken with before.

"Who is this?" I asked, playing along. "Chris McCandless?"

"Yes, it's me," Ang answered.

"Yeah, right," I respond with dubiousness. "How do I know it's you?"

"Ask me anything."

"Okay," I said, rubbing my chin. "Where did you go to school?"

"Which one?" she asked. "I went to Woodson High School in Fairfax, Virginia and graduated from Emory University with two bachelors in history and anthropology."

"What's your sister's name?"

"Carine."

"Didn't you change your name at some point?"

"Alexander Supertramp."

My eyebrows shot up in surprise. "Yeah," I smiled, "that's a doozy. Where'd your father work?"

"NASA," she answered, and then added, "My mother worked at Hughes Aircraft."

"This is incredible," I said. "I don't see how an old woman from a rez would know all this, but I guess it's you. Where are you right now?"

"The other side," she answered simply.

"Where is that?" I asked.

"Everywhere," she said. "Souls are boundless and not restrained by space and time."

"I don't know what all that means, but whatever. So, how are you feeling?"

"Can't complain," she responded.

"You know they made a movie about you, right?"

"Yes. I've seen it?"

"Really? What do you have over there on the other side, like, cable or something?"

"Something like that. It was a Sean Penn flick, right?"

"Yeah," I retorted. "Emile Hirsch played you."

"He did a fine job, too, but I'm bigger than that."

"What do you mean?" I asked. "You're taller than Emile? Heavier?"

"No. Remember that scene where I was supposedly floating naked in the river? That overhead shot where you could see everything?"

"Yeah."

"Well, I'm bigger than what they showed."

"Um, Chris, I don't think that's important."

"Yeah, I know. But they could at least get the details right."

"Chris," I uttered, "I'm writing a book about what it's like to be homeless. You ran so far away from society, I just wanted to know what that felt like."

"I have a curious mind," she began. "When I went to bed at night I never really had a full sleep because my mind was going at 100mph. All these thoughts, colliding like insects caught in a net. Really hard to focus on just one, you know? I don't know, man, I just had to get out, you know, like free myself somehow?"

"I understand. So, what was Alaska like?"

"Lonely. And cold."

"Anything special happened?"

"I died."

"Yeah, um, I mean besides that."

"Well, you know, every day was basically the same thing – wake up, forage for food, nap, forage for food, read a book, forage for food, make some entries in my journal, forage for food…"

"Yeah, Chris," I interrupted, "I mean, did you have an epiphany or come to a revelation?"

"You mean, like, did I see a heavenly light?"

"Yeah. Let's go with that."

"Nah. Of course, every day, I thought I should just give up this wild idea and go back home. It's so strange, you know. Once I've set my mind on doing something, you can etch it in marble."

"Was it like you thought it'd be?"

"Yep. I knew what I was in for."

"You had doubts?"

"Of course. I think anyone would. You've spent your whole life around people you love, and sometimes people you can't stand, but in its own way it keeps you alive. I just...Robin, you're familiar with Supertramp, right?"

"The band?" I asked. "Oh, yeah. Breakfast in America is one of my favorite albums. It was actually one of six albums I won for being the sixth caller to some radio station in New York, probably WNBC 66 or something. It was a long time ago."

"Yeah, I know that album. Good one. Are you familiar with their earlier one, Crime of the Century?"

"A little."

"There's a song on there," she elucidated, "the title track. The words go like this:

"Now they're planning the crime of the century / Well what will it be? / Read all about their schemes and adventuring / It's well worth a fee / So roll up and see / And they rape the universe / How they've gone from bad to worse / Who are these men of lust, greed and glory? / Rip off the masks and let's see / But that's not right / Oh no, what's the story / there's you and there's me / That can't be right."

"See, Robin? These men of lust, greed and glory are all of us. We want more, we want the best. We've gotta have the biggest house on the block, the best car in the garage, the fattest bank account in town...when does it end? Does it really make us happy, all that excess? When we think we've got want we want, we want more. All greed does is taint us, man. It made me feel dirty, anyway. I looked around and saw what I didn't want to become, some greedy unsatisfiable bloodless parasite just sucking out the marrow of a cancerous bone called modern society. That's living? That's just trying to be one up on the next man, and it's all for nothing. Working that hard...for nothing. I...I didn't want any parts of it, man. That's why I broke free."

"Sounds...noble," I managed to say though I wasn't sure if that was the right word. "So," I continued, "did you ultimately find what you were looking for?"

"I ran out of time," he admitted. "I wasn't prepared."

"Yeah. You know, there are two schools of thought concerning that trip."

"I'm aware," she explained. "Those who think I had the right idea but just the wrong venue and those who see me as just some idealistic but immature, narcissistic fool."

"Yes," I surmised, "to some people you're a folk hero. They make treks all the way up the Stampede Trail to see the magic bus. A lot of kids got turned on to Jack London, too, because he's one of your favorite authors."

"Me and Jack have a lot in common," she revealed. "We're both free-spirited guys from California, we both died young, tramped around the country, we're both writers even though I never published my stories…"

"I didn't know you wrote."

"Sure," she stated. "I wrote a bunch of stories in Emory, but I don't know, I didn't think they were that good."

"Well, it's a good thing you didn't choose that path."

"What do you mean?"

"You said you can't write."

"I didn't say I can't write!" she blurted. "I just didn't think they were that good!"

"Okay, okay, sorry," I apologized. "You know, you're pretty sensitive."

"It's okay, man. I've been kinda stressed lately."

"About what?"

Just as I thought she was about to answer, Madame Ang stretched her arms out to the side and gave a big yawn.

"You sound tired," I remarked.

"I'm not," she answered, "but this fortune teller is. I think I'd better bring her back."

"Okay," I said reluctantly. "It was nice talking to you, Chris, Alexander Supertramp."

"My pleasure."

"Hey, Chris," I wondered, "does everyone who die end up on the other side?"

"Uh, huh," he answered. "The body's just a vessel for the soul. The soul is infinite."

"Oh, yeah?" I exhorted happily. "I've been reading all about that lately."

"Reading all about what?" Madame Ang, finally opening her eyes, asked with her old, gravelly voice.

"Do you remember anything we talked about?" I asked.

"Nothing," she replied. "I'm just a conduit."

"Yeah," I shook my head. "I guess you are."

"Did you find what you were looking for, like answers?"

"Yes," I answered. "It was pretty helpful. You really don't remember anything?"

"Not a word."

"Well," I said, standing up and offering her my hand, "it was an interesting experience, to say the least."

"My pleasure."

"I think I'll go home," I rationalized, "'cause the rain has stopped."

"What rain?" she asked.

"Are you kidding?" I asked dubiously. "It's cats and dogs out there."

To emphasize my point, I opened the door wide enough so we both could look out. My jaw dropped. Not only was there no rain but the ground was as dry as the Sahara.

"This can't be." I declared. "There was a downpour a short while ago."

Madame Ang walked over, put one hand on my shoulder, and said, "There's an old Cherokee saying: We do not create stories; sometimes the old ones allow themselves to be revealed."

"I don't know what that means," I admitted, "but thanks for everything."

"Will you come back again?" she asked.

I looked at her and nodded. "I think you already know the answer."

***

Singer, songwriter, guitarist, fellow Pacific Northwest resident Steve Miller currently has his sprawling estate on San Juan Islands up for grabs. If you've got $16M, it's yours, no questions asked. You can get there by ferry or seaplane if you want to check it out. By seaplane it takes about 40 minutes from Seattle. If you prefer sticking close to the land, you have to drive about 70 minutes up I-5 to Anacortes and take the ferry from there. I'd go check out the mansion myself but I kinda forget where I left that $16M I'd found in the street last week.

Brother Steve is one of the good guys. He even wrote a song for us, the disenfranchised, called "Fly Like an Eagle." To wit:

"Feed the babies who don't have enough to eat. Shoe the children with no shoes on their feet. House the people living in the streets. Oh, oh, there's a solution."

Kinda funny that Steve should say there's a solution because, believe it or not, I have one. As soon as I'm done here I'm gonna call him up in San Juan and tell him the solution is to house those people living in the streets in the massive mansion he has up for grabs. C'mon, Brother Steve. I know you have an altruistic spirit. Show the world how much you care. Don't make a liar out of me.

CHAPTER 11
Ekatva – The Jain Concept *of* Being Alone

"I have a son who is a...not an ordinary form of schizophrenia, but clearly, cannot take care of himself. And the great fear of then, of all parents is, when the parents die, who takes care of your child? And the answer is: they become homeless." James D. Watson, American molecular biologist, geneticist and zoologist.

Official Definition of Jainism: Jainism is an ancient religion from India that teaches the way to liberation and bliss is to live a life of harmlessness and renunciation. The aim of Jain life is to achieve liberation of the soul. Ahimsa, non-violence, is first and foremost of all Jain beliefs.

Robin's Simple Definition of Jainism: *Own nothing, want nothing, harm nothing.*

"Nobody can suffer the fruits of another person's good or bad deeds (karmas). We enter the world and leave it alone." Tattvartha Sutra

From the outside, Jainism looks like a strict religion with lots of rules and, therefore, happiness could never factor into its practice. But just think about this for a minute: if you own nothing or very little, you'll have very low anxiety about people stealing or destroying your stuff. That's freedom. If you don't desire your neighbor's three-bedroom colonial, your cousin's Mercedes Benz, your brother's model wife or Mark Zuckerberg's gold debit card, there's no stress because you're not breaking your back trying to get those things. That's freedom. If you severely reduce your diet to just fruits and vegetables, and therefore avoiding harm to all animals, your mind & body will thank you for the restraint and you don't have to waste your precious time and hard earned money trying to lose weight in a gym or paying for expensive medicines for diseases which are preventable from having a healthy body, like diabetes, obesity, high blood pressure, strokes, etc.

That's freedom, and freedom is happiness.

So, what does Jainism have to do with being homeless? Society may think homelessness is an extremely bad situation, which it is, but Jainism supports you by saying it's okay to desire very little and what you are doing is virtuous and not to be ridiculed. You don't have a house? That's okay. You can go ahead and tell the mortgage banks thanks, but no thanks. You don't have a car? No problem. The price of gas is too high anyway so you can write to Exxon and tell them it's been real.

Being homeless also means you have very little articles of clothing, unless you walk around town with your Ikea closet on a cart. But for those of us who are not that fortunate, Jainism says it's okay to have very little clothes. Some of our monks have no clothes at all; they walk around naked like the prophet whose teachings we follow, Mahavir. Of course, you can't walk around naked in America. Not only will you be arrested, but here in Seattle, you'll also have to register as a sex offender. It's already bad enough having to look upon a scraggly, dirty homeless man; but having to look upon a scraggly, dirty, *naked* homeless man might be more torture than American society can bear. Just so you readers know: I'm not proselytizing Jainism. That's not my style. Everyone has a right to follow their own beliefs. I just happen to live as minimally as possible, and as it turns out, Jainism's got my back on that. I can't complain.

***

I saw some promising news this morning. Cities like Houston, Los Angeles and San Francisco are stepping up their efforts to house the homeless as well as offer coordinated care with this population's addictions and mental illnesses. I hope it's not just empty rhetoric to appease those who've had it up to here with RV's parked in front of their homes. Time will tell how successful these new initiatives are. Maybe in ten years, books like these wouldn't have to be written.

CHAPTER 12
Cuddle, Cuddle Toil *and* Trouble

"No one is asking what happened to all the homeless. No one cares, because it's easier to get on the subway and not be accosted." Richard Linklater, filmmaker/screenwriter/actor.

Let me begin by saying this chapter is not about rape. Rape is not a crime of passion, it is a crime of evil. Plain and simple. I don't condone it and abhor anyone who participates in it. Does anyone remember Maine congressman Lawrence Lockman? Among all the divisive comments he's made over the years, he had this doozy: "If a woman has the right to abortion, why shouldn't a man be free to use his superior strength to force himself on a woman? At least the rapist's pursuit of sexual freedom doesn't, in most cases, result in anyone's death." Sexual freedom? Is this guy insane? Sexual freedom is being able to fancy who you want, not forcing yourself onto someone else.

Most people want to love and be loved, to care and be cared for, to entertain and be entertained, to house and be housed. Of course, there are those amongst us who don't give a rat's posterior to all these contrivances, but this chapter isn't for them. In fact, I'm confident they wouldn't be thumbing through this book anyway since, within these pages, there are no lessons on how to skin your fellow man or pluck his nerves like they're the strings of a ukulele. This chapter is for those of us who weren't that fortunate in the looks department and possess the magnetic attractiveness of a falling sledgehammer.

Have you ever sat in a park eating vegetable chow mein with chopsticks only to get momentarily distracted by Quasimodo walking hand in hand with Sleeping Beauty right in front of you? It makes you think, "Gee, what does he have that I don't have?" Hey, maybe Superboy is rich, or charming, or says the right things, or has a nice pad, or is chivalrous enough to open doors for his paramour and lay down in a puddle of mud so she can walk over him to safety. In all reality, there may not even be one or two particular reasons. It could've been they simply found each other at a low point in their lives, clicked, and decided to spend their time together. Whether by luck or design, they found each other. If they make their relationship work, even better.

But what happens when you're getting old, time is passing you by, you're lonely as hell, that Good Ship Lollipop has sailed on by and you're stuck on the shore watching your dreams sail over the horizon? Do you keep your hopes up or just fuggedaboutit? Here are a few stats to ponder: 18% of men and 12% of women in the U.S. go to their graves without ever getting married. In the U.S., 5% of men and 2% of women go to their graves as virgins; that's roughly 16 million men and 6 ½ million women who've never had amorous congress, boinked, stuffed the muffin or, as they say in Germany, blitzkrieg mit dem fleischgewehr. The truth is, some people get lucky at a young age while others don't find Mr. or Mrs. Right till they're in their 50's, 60's, 70's or more. The internet if filled with these kinds of stories. Just look, you'll see.

Of course, sex is such a broad term that it's sometimes debatable what constitutes buzzing the Brillo. Is a hand job sex? What about a pipe job? Sea food dinner? Fornicating by cigar? If sexual intercourse is, according to Google, simply penetration by a man into a woman's holiest of holies, then at 53 years old, I'm still a virgin. If sex constitutes all the variations I just mentioned, and then some, then I'm not a virgin. Obviously, my scant history in this aspect of human development does not make me Dr. Ruth Westheimer or Alfred Kinsey, but I do know a little bit about winning people over.

Be nice. It never hurts to compliment someone, not interrupt them when they're speaking, pay close attention to the words coming out of their mouth, offer them help with simple tasks, or ask them how their day has been. People love attention, and I should know. I'm a clown and clowns love attention (just not the bad kind). I once made an error by telling someone they looked particularly ravishing when, in reality, they were hung over and looked like they just went ten rounds with Kimbo Slice. As a result, they told me to stop patronizing them. Okay. Lesson learned. Next time I'll just ask, "Is there something I can get for you? Dialysis? A blood transfusion? A gallon of V8 and a nasogastric tube to spare you the trouble of drinking it?" In the past, I've found simple questions such as, "Would you like some company?" to be very helpful in breaking the ice. The worst they can say is "Get lost!" The best they can say is, "Sure." As Jamaicans say, "Nothin' try, nothin' done."

Give presents. I love gifts, especially those with dead presidents attached to them. Whether it is chocolates, candies, clothes, unleaded gas, whatever, a gift is a gift. It means someone is thinking about you, someone has you in mind, and that's a good feeling. If you want to show the object of your affection that they hold some meaning to you, and you have nary a doubloon in ye pockets, don't stress. You can still get them things for free. BTW, here's a tip: if they don't appreciate your free presents, they're not worth the time and effort anyway because such people will never be pleased by you.

If you have food stamps you get always get someone cheese. Most people I know love cheese, with string cheese being their favorite. Pepperidge Farm cookies are pretty good, too, especially those with strawberry or apricot jelly in the middle. Totally dry cookies make me choke to death. Wouldn't it be a drag that you brought someone you like a bag of cookies only to spend the next five minutes administering CPR bringing them back to life? Wine and beer are good presents too, but you can't buy those with food stamps. You can, however, get creative and buy the ingredients required to make pruno. Pruno, for those of you who've never done time in a federal penitentiary, is prison wine made from apples, oranges, milk, ketchup, sugar and whatever else the rats dragged in. You add water to that crazy-ass mixture, place it in a plastic bag or, if you're lucky, an empty Clorox bottle, wrap it with a pillow case, and just let it ferment over the next week or two in a cool, dry place. What you'll end up with is a drink that looks and tastes exactly like camel vomit, but since the alcohol content will be as high as Thunderbird, you won't care or even notice.

If you absolutely, positively must give someone a present and you've forgotten what currency looks like because you haven't see it in so long, don't fret. Robin has you covered. For one, feel free to visit the various food banks around town. You'd be surprised what they give away sometimes. During the Christmas season, some give away whole tins of Black Forest ham; during Thanksgiving, it's Butterball turkey. Yes, this is useless if you don't have an oven to bake it in, but since a lot of parks have outdoor ovens in them, that's always an option. Food banks, from time to time, also dole out confectionaries like pies, cakes and biscuits that are maybe only three or four days old, so choose wisely.

Another place to look for free stuff is the various social service agencies and missions around town. I've gotten socks, blankets, hats and scarves from them. They're all usually second hand except the socks, but they're all clean…for the most part. Still, I have yet to see a blanket being given away with a piss stain so large it looked like it was kept in the horse stable at Griffith Park. Walking around well-to-do neighborhoods sometimes yield some interesting treasures, too. Just yesterday I found a pair of computer speakers sitting in a roundabout. I haven't tested them yet, but since they were left out in public, they most likely work otherwise they would've been chucked in a bin a long time ago. Office chairs are also a popular find. Some might be missing an armrest, but that's a minor issue. I've also found lamps, flashlights, sun glasses, cell phones, book cases, car wax, couches, center tables, corner tables, computer hutches, seizure helmets, pens, books, you name it. You never know what you'll find out there.

Time. Yep, your time is a gift. Nothing says "you matter to me" more than the gift of your time. What y'all do in your free time is completely up to you, but in this busy super-industrialized world, time is a commodity. This is a little cheesy, but if you were to make up your own ticket with the words *"The bearer of this ticket gets free hugs from _____" or "…free uninterrupted time from_____",* it'll be greatly appreciated by its recipient. And again, if they don't appreciate the gesture, then I know over 100 ways to say sayonara. Just ask.

Learn What Floats their Boats. Nothing will kill a conversation faster than both parties having absolutely nothing in common. Bob likes deep sea fishing but Mary hates water. Bob loves BBQ ribs, pan-seared chicken breast with shallots, and Mississippi coon stew (yeah, it's what you think it is). Mary detests all types of meat and prefers kale & arugula salads for lunch and, at dinner, she's a sucker for tofu & mushroom miso soup, chickpea curry with basmati rice, vegan tofu ceviche or Kung Pao tofu with Chinese broccoli and brown rice. Bob loves movies where tendons and cartilage get yanked out by rusty pruning tools while Mary would rather crazy glue her eyelids shut that sit through a gruesome blood fest. If her flicks aren't Disney or Pixar productions, don't waste her time. Bob loves most sports – hockey, basketball, football, baseball, rugby, soccer, etc. Mary would rather spend her time knitting blankets, making bracelets and chains out of buttons and beads, or folding ordinary pieces of paper into dragons, chickens and roses. When it comes to music it's thrash or black metal for Bob and Katy Perry or Beyoncé for Mary. Bob is pretty laid back and takes everything in stride; Mary is a worrywart, the Queen of Complaints. Heaven forbid she should walk into a bathroom and discover the roll of toilet paper is hung upside down or there's water splashed on the mirror.

The chance of Bob and Mary hitting it off smoothly is practically nil. Compromises would have to be made. It's only fair that both parties would have to bend over backwards a little if they want a relationship to work. This is where a lot of couples run into trouble. One person gives 95% vs. the other person's 5% to the union. An imbalance like that means their relationship is doomed to fail. Should Mary watch movies that'll give her nightmares or Bob sit through rated G fare that could make him lapse into a coma? Since there is no such film like The Lion King vs. Predator, that means it's time to scour internet movie review sites like IMDb or Rotten Tomatoes to find out what's worth watching. You can either trust a film's high rating that it might be worthwhile or just wing it and go with something that contains some element of what you both like. If you can think it, it probably exists. It may be a foreign language film, but a little subtitle reading never killed anyone.

Honesty goes a long way in building formidable relationships. It should be okay to say to someone you fancy, "I don't care for this or that; however, I'll do it for you if you're willing to do this or that for me." I think that's pretty fair. A little open-mindedness is often required to make a partnership work. I had a friend who once said to me, "Hey, let's go feed the ducks." The first that came to my mind was jumping out the window and getting away as far as I could. Me? Sit on the bank of some quiet, fog-skimmed lake throwing bits of wheat bread to ducks I'd prefer see hanging up over a spinning spit or displayed on my plate Peking style? No thanks. But, to keep the peace, I indulged her. And I enjoyed it; that was a pleasant surprise. I've since come to view ducks as being very intelligent animals, not just greedy birds flooding the lakes with poop. Again, compromises and sacrifices made by both parties are important. I've made the mistake of "buying" relationships in the past and they all failed. Lesson learned: you can't buy a partner. They have to meet you half way.

CHAPTER 13
Volunteering *in* Your Neighborhood

"I guess because I had such a horrible life growing up, going from place to place, not knowing what I was gonna do and ending up being homeless, there was a lot of pain and a lot of anger that was coming out through my guitar playing." Dave Mustaine, Megadeth.

If you have the time, and the inclination, then volunteering your time is an excellent way to keep from going crazy with boredom. If you're a raging alcoholic or drug addict, obviously, this chapter doesn't apply because you're already too busy looking for your next blast or drink or whatever. Volunteering is also a good way to show the world that the homeless aren't so bad; as it is, threats or actual cuts in federal social programs continues to plague this community. I've always looked at it this way: one less homeless person on the street, one less person trying to break into your car or house.

Food Banks. Great place to volunteer, maybe even the #1 place. If they need the help, you can do things like take applications for social services, stack shelves with food, do maintenance work if that's your thing, wash fruits and vegetables, or distribute food products to the needy. Some of the bigger banks have their own trucks so you can always go along for the ride to acquire foodstuffs to help your fellow poor. Food banks are also a good place to meet like-minded people, too. You're all in the same boat, just trying your best to scrape by. It's always a plus to be able to trade your tales of desperation; you'll make new friends, gain community and start to develop a network of folks who may be able to help you out with your plight.

Community Centers. There's one in this town where I volunteer to do the dishes. They reward me by letting me use their washer and dryer for free or feeding me lunch. From time to time I also clean the bathrooms. Have you ever seen a bathroom just after a man with Parkinson's and dementia used it? It makes downtown Fallujah look like Martha's Vineyard. Another plus that comes with volunteering at a community center is you get a chance to heat up your food in a microwave if they have one. Eating pork & beans, turkey chili and Manhattan clam chowder right out of a can does sustain life, but in case you've forgotten, they do taste better heated. Some community centers also help with job and skills training, including how to show people where the 'On' button on a computer is. Those of you who were laid off from their clerical job at Amazon can put some of those skills to work here – typing letters, teaching folks Excel and Word, and maybe even how to load the complicated, newfangled staplers. Who designed those? Stephen Hawking?

Animal Shelters. If pitbulls don't scare you to death like they do me, animal shelters are also cool places to spend your time. Volunteers do a variety of things there such as washing down cages, feeding and cleaning the animals, picking strays up from the street and doing general maintenance of the shelter. I did this during that summer when "My Sharona" by The Knack was the number one hit on FM. (That's radio, for those of you who grew up in the internet era). If you have a soft heart for cats, dogs and bunnies then animal shelters are the way to go. As a side note, I do feel bad to this very day that I turned a cat into the shelter when I had to abandon the apartment I'd lived in for 8 years. The cat, Missy, was a stray but kept me company for the last two years I was domiciled. I'd seen reports on TV that stray cats are bad news for suburban neighborhoods because they're notorious killers of the animals that live naturally there, like birds and squirrels, and are a nuisance because the odor of their pee and poop can chip paint off a wall. They're noisy, especially at night, and they often fight with Mrs. Annie's Russian Blue cat whenever she goes outside for a little air and sunshine. Not good.

Libraries. These are good places if, like me, you're addicted to the written language. Stacking books and magazines is fun, and so are writing reviews, designing posters, helping with general clerical assistance, reading to young kids and perhaps even tutoring those in danger of getting left behind. It's a good place for reprieve from the elements, too. Who wants to spend the entire day baking in the sun? They're also a cool place for meeting new people, too.

Hospitals & Nursing Homes. If the smell of blood and bedpans doesn't bother you, then these places may be of interest. Remember the candy stripers back in the day, those girls and grown women dressed in pink and white striped dresses who assisted in these medical centers? Their job was to read to the elderly patients, deliver magazines to them, comfort them and perhaps even report to the staff that something doesn't look right with them. In some nursing homes the volunteers are allowed to bring snacks and drinks to the patients. They're not allowed to feed them though, just in case that Oreo goes down sideways and Mr. Fields now has to fight just to catch a breath. Hospitals, being larger institutions than nursing homes, have a lot more opportunities for volunteers, from directing visitors to the right floor to helping comfort patients by visiting them with dogs or cats. I don't think any hospital would let you visit rooms and put on a Patch Adams type of show, though. If Mr. Fields has a heart attack because of you, the insurance premium at the hospital will go through the roof. If you can sing or play guitar, that could also come in handy for entertaining patients. But use common sense. You can't go into a nursing home and start singing Slipknot. You'll end up flooding the parking lot with emergency vehicles and the Direct of Nursing won't be so pleased with you.

Parks & Recreation. There you go. You get a chance to help your fellow homeless by cleaning up the trash and needles and broken glass bubbles they've strewn all over the place. Here in Seattle, some of the greenbelts are littered to the point of being just one spray can away of qualifying as landfills. The homeless do have to sleep somewhere, and the drug addicts do have to shoot up somewhere; unfortunately, many of them don't bother cleaning up after themselves. The result? Poop, plastic bags, abandoned tents, beer cans, beer bottles, whiskey bottles, tourniquets, empty food wrappers and radios with their guts ripped out lying all over the place. Giving back this way is a prime opportunity to show that not all homeless people are dirty, so the government can go ahead and get rid of that rusty old barge sitting at the Puget Sound pier. We're not getting on it to sail to China like City Council wants us to. If you want to you can always call or write to the powers that be at City Hall to send a crew out to a compromised site. It's a coordinated effort to clean up an encampment so a few departments have to be on the same page on the same day at the same time - Parks & Recreation, Hazardous Materials, Social Workers and the Porta John people.

***

I went into QFC this morning to buy my usual breakfast: bagel with cream cheese and an orange soda. Then, as I was about to go upstairs to the sitting area, I stopped and glanced at the Seattle Times. Call me nosy but, every once in a while, I do like to know what's going on in the world. You never know. There could be a zombie apocalypse taking place in Portland. I think it's better to be prepared just in case the undead infection spreads out to the rest of the cities in the Pacific Northwest. Talking about zombie apocalypse, this brings me to this morning's observation – how the media fans the flames of hatred and divisiveness to make money.

The headline I'd read said, "From ocean to Idaho border, state becoming less white." Now the question is, "Why is this so important to know that it warrants a broadcast?" Remember the firefighter who started fires because his station was facing budget cuts and was in danger of closing so he had to show that, yes, firefighters are needed?" Same principle here: the media is in the business of making money; that's their bottom line. The more sensational the news, the better. Blood sells newspapers because it piques people's curiosity enough for them to look into the various media outlets for information, and that translates into increased ad revenue. If there's a tsunami, a few people want to read about it. If there's a tsunami so large that it's engulfing the entire western seaboard, a lot of people want to read about it. The problem here is that the more ignorant among us falls for the media's slant; if it's in print, it must be important.

Okay, so from ocean to Idaho border, state becoming less white. Why is this important to know? Is the Seattle Times hoping that the more militant among us take to arms because their precious land is being invaded? If there is a run on guns, will said guns be used? Can this begin a "gasp!" race war? Does that mean there will be blood on the street? Sweet! People will want to read about it so they'll turn to the media for more info. Does the media care if there's a race war and people are fighting in the street? Hell no. The media moguls will simply chill in their protected gated homes watching the fracas from the safety of their cozy living rooms while cities are going up in flames. They could care less. No wonder they spend so much time writing about the homeless: we're opposite to the norm, which means we're antagonists, which means we have to be controlled and monitored because we're scary, which means the citizenry should arm themselves and attack us like in Ironweed, which means blood in the streets, which means increased revenue from increased readership, which means new yacht in the mogul's marina. I'm not fooled. I hope others aren't, either.

CHAPTER 14
Seattle Five-*0*

"You know, if I listened to Michael Dukakis long enough, I would be convinced we're in an economic downturn and people are homeless and going without food and medical attention and that we've got to do something about the unemployed." Ronald Reagan, President of the United States, 1981-1989.

Contrary to popular opinion, and I'll probably get my hide flayed for this, the police are your friend. Like grocery store owners and park rangers, they're just doing their job. True, some do get out of hand and need discipline – they're only human even though they're deadly humans – still, they do come in handy sometimes, like when Big Bad Bill decides one particularly cold night to swipe your blanket and, because he's 6'6" tall and 275lbs, too big to beat.

During my "bad" days I tried to avoid the police at all costs, after all, their job was to get miscreants like me off the street so the rest of America can sleep soundly and peacefully in their warm, comfortable beds. It was a constant cat and mouse game; I was always on the hunt for this and that, and they were on the hunt for me. Yes, there were times I would've liked to approach them to complain that my money was robbed by a dealer, but of course, they'd just shake their heads and say, "Asshole." I suppose I could've armed myself like a lot of addicts do, but since violence was not part and parcel of what constitutes me, I never did. The police have always had a bad rap especially in regards to minorities. Now that the "Black Lives Matter" movement is in full swing, their reputation for "shoot first, ask questions later" has taken center stage. At this point it behooves them to counter all the negativity swirling around by holding community sessions and fielding questions from the general pop. It couldn't hurt. So, with that in mind, how can the police help the homeless? Well, I'm glad you asked.

Stop harassing us. Who in their right mind would choose to live right out in the open, under the elements, dragging their dirty carcass all around town just looking for a bite to eat? It's bad enough that people look at us like we just ran over their precious puppy; I mean, how much lower can our self-esteem get? No one likes to hear, "Get up! You can't sleep here!" How'd you like it if we sneaked into your bedroom in the middle of the night, tapped loudly on your dresser with our flashlights, shined the bright light in your eyes, and ordered you to get up? Chances are you'd whip out a gun and but a bullet in our chests so fast you'd make Annie Oakley look like a quad. A little respect, please.

Help us. Yep. Provide us with lists of places where we can eat, take a shower, get new clothes, take a load off, watch the general election, etc. Just because we're on the street doesn't mean we have no vested interest in what transpires from the Atlantic to the Pacific and beyond. We do care; most of us just don't show it because, physically, we're too beat to give our opinions. Yes, some of us are also way too high to render a coherent point, but that's another matter altogether. I suppose it'd be too much to ask to give us rides to community centers and the like, but I think every so often it wouldn't kill you to stop and ask if we need any help. As you cruise around, you'll notice that some of our less fortunate brothers and sisters are not, how shall I say, well put together. I suppose as long as they're not hurting people, what harm is it having them roam the streets. In my opinion, and I do have a few, some people just don't know how to ask for help. I'm not saying you should just roll up and drag someone off to a hospital, but it might help to have professionals evaluate them to see if there's anything the city can do to ease their pain of living on the street. Contrary to popular belief, not everyone likes living in the gutters. Some of us are looking at the stars. I can tell you that from experience.

Support us. You have a voice, a very powerful voice in society. Congressmen, the mayor, city council members, and other elected dignitaries will listen to you because you encounter us every day. You're down deep in the jungle with us, mixing in like wildebeests among the wolves. When you see us sleeping in abandoned buildings, please, don't tell us to go. Where would we go? To another abandoned building? Don't you get tired of chasing us from site to site? Maybe you can encourage Parks and Recreation to leave Honey Buckets in the woods near our campsites so we wouldn't have to pollute the land with our toxic wastes. And encourage City Light to leave the electricity on in places where we can plug in our coffee makers and cellphones, like public parks and recreation centers. And if we call for help, please, don't just say you'll be right there but then never show up. That's just disrespectful. I'd rather you just say, "Eh, you're homeless. We're not coming," than insist that you are. That's troubling.

Ask us. We don't bite. (Hell, most of us don't have teeth anyway). Isn't it interesting that, every time you look in the newspaper, you see this policy maker and that ombudsman advocating for the homeless like they know us better than their own children? It really makes you wonder if people really care or it's just a paycheck, like scrubbing elephants at a zoo or pouring hot lattes at Tully's. Here's a better suggestion: ask the homeless how best to help the homeless. We're not slow; we do have answers but no one asks us. We don't want to be on the street. We want homes, too. We want to live again, laugh again, enjoy the sunshine like everyone else, not hide in the shadows like rats on a listing galleon. Homeless Harry is standing by waiting for your call. I promise you, he won't bite.

Listen to us. I can't lie – the police barracks around here are beautiful to the eyes, modern works of exemplary design and craftsmanship. So, it does us no good when we come to you for help or to lodge a complaint that you just talk to us through the box on the outside wall. I know you want to weed out the wheat from the chaff but I don't seriously believe anyone would go out of their way to approach the police, given your local reputation. But I know what you're thinking: "You can't be too careful these days." I respect that. The bottom line is we mean you no harm just as much as we hope you don't mean us harm. Fair enough?

CHAPTER 15
Purple Haze, Brown Sugar *and* White Lines

"I've lived in many things – boats, caravans and buses. I've been homeless. I've had no money: everything. But I believe in magic, and having a vision. The tough times made me a warrior. I work hard."
Neon Hitch, singer.

I have yet to find a metropolitan city where illicit pharmaceuticals aren't a problem. Is America losing its war on drugs? Yes, I know, I'm the last person to talk about drug control given my history – 22 years of abusing it. I'm one of the lucky ones who never got caught and went to jail, but as they say in the rooms, that's a "yet." I have ripped open my right palm jumping over a fence to elude the police in Hollywood, hospitalized a few times for extreme paranoia and overdoses, hospitalized for a suicide attempt, hanged around some of the most dangerous people I could find - drug dealers, Mexican gang members, murderers, rapists, prostitutes, bail jumpers, and walked into neighborhoods that, technically, I shouldn't have been able to walk out of. So, without sounding like a hypocrite, I'll try my best not to point a finger at Afghanistan, Mexico or the American legal system but, instead, focus on its impact re: the homeless.

Out on the street, if you have money, you have friends. They don't care how short or tall or fat or straight or gay or twisted or black or white or how poorly dressed you are. They don't even care if you get naked every night and swing off the chandelier in the rotunda of City Hall with the Backstreet Boys playing on a boombox on the floor. On the street, money talks, bullshit hits the highway. When you're an addict, you can care less about the environment or who the new president is. That festering sore on your ankle will have to take a backseat to a fix. You look so different now that, if your own children you left behind passed you on the street, they wouldn't know you from Santa's elves.

I envy people who tried this or that drug then said, "Nope. That's not for me." I think there must be more to it than a simple "I didn't like how it made me feel." I suppose everyone has a different body chemistry, and as such, drugs affect us all differently. But what persuades someone to keep on using and using till their teeth fall out, till they get a heart attack, till they end up in prison for bank robbery, till they push a steak knife through a dealer's ribs for his stash? Wouldn't be nice if the answer was as simple as, "Johnny's hooked on drugs because his father beat him?"

As it turns out, the brain loves dopamine. Can't get enough of it. The acts of eating and fornicating drips a little bit of dopamine, a neurotransmitter synthesized by the brain, into other parts of the brain that craves it, those parts that say, "I want this body I live in to thrive and procreate. I don't care if this body climbs Mt. Everest or has an Oprah Winfrey fetish. Just give me dopamine, dammit; everything else is bullshit." When drugs are introduced, the brain says, "Wow. Forget the hamburger and the sex. Just give me more dopamine." What an anomaly – the brain hijacking itself.

No one in this society is immune to the effects of drug abuse. It doesn't matter if you can't tell a barbiturate from a can of peas, but if someone in your family is addicted, keep your jewelry and silverware in site at all times. As a matter of fact, anchor your LED TV to the wall and add automatic flame throwers to your smartphone. You're gonna need it. Needle Nellie isn't gonna stop till she digs up something in the house she can sell at the nearest pawn shop.

You know, it was only going to be a matter of time when they legalized weed. I didn't think I'd see it in my lifetime, but here it is. Bob Marley's dream came true. There are more recreational drug stores in Seattle than Chinese restaurants; good if you love sativa, bad if you love shrimp toast. Cocaine, heroin, shrooms, acid, Ecstasy, wax (marijuana whose THC content can be as high as 88%), glass, Georgia Home Boy, whatever, aren't legal…yet. Won't happen in my lifetime, though. I'll be worm food by the time they even get around to consider legalizing those.

What an interesting evolution man has been through these past, oh, 300,000 years or so. Back then things were very simple – eat or be eaten, strike or be stricken. No time clocks to punch, no gas tanks to fill, no electricity to pay. Were we supposed to evolve to this point of leisure, where we don't have to look over our shoulders every minute of the day? Maybe in 1,000 years they'll look back at these times and say, "Wow, was the earth in shambles back then!" It'd be nice if I could live to 1,000 years or more. I guess it doesn't matter. Every generation brings new problems. Among other issues, like terrorist attacks, climate warming and equal rights, drug abuse is one of the biggest. My brothers and sisters on the street use it…a lot. Let's see if we can find out why they're there, how they got there, and offer some help; the present is a good time to start.

CHAPTER 16
Sloshed, Smashed *and* Snookered

"Starbucks is the last public space with chairs. It's a shower for homeless people. And it's a place you can write all day. The baristas don't glare at you. They don't even look at you." Mike Birbiglia, comedian/actor/ writer/director.

What can be said? Alcohol to the homeless is like Kryptonite to Superman – it's in our DNA but it can kill us when overly exposed to it. Isn't that horrible? Normal people can have a sip or two of Chianti Riserva with their dinner of Paella Marinera or Table de Queso, then stand around all night talking about skiing in Aspen or retiring in the South of France. Alcohol to a lot of homeless people doesn't seem like a choice; really, it's more like a necessity, as if needed just to see the whole day through in one piece. Yeah, it can be a panacea for what ails you – at first – then it slowly creeps up on you like a demon spawn, threatening to drag you through the darkest depths of Hell with its long, unwavering, unapologetic fingers. Alcohol is a bane and a curse to those of us predisposed to addiction. If you don't have a problem with stopping, that's good. It's honorable, really. Sure wish I was one of those people.

Alcoholism and addiction runs in my family. My paternal grandfather smoked opium when he came home after a long week at work from the Chinese restaurant he co-owned. I don't know if he drank liquor, though. At least I never saw that anyway. One night, I accidentally went into his bedroom. Silly me. He could've been knocking boots with his wife (unrelated to me) but, instead, he was simply lying on his side in a room that was full of white odorless smoke. It wasn't until years later when I realized what he was doing. Apparently, opium was popular with the Chinese back in the day and my grandfather, himself Cantonese, was no exception.

My father was the worst alcoholic ever. They say there are four types of alcoholics – the lovers, the sleepers, the fighters and the clowns. My main trait when I drank was being a clown. My father, however, was the fighter. When I think about it, I don't believe I ever saw him sober when I was a kid. I barely talked to him, anyway. He wasn't the kind of man you sparred words with. Sorry, ain't gonna happen unless you don't mind spitting out your teeth. Any conversation with my father was nothing more than cruising for a bruising. He used to sit around the house with his dark shades on with a newspaper in his hands. The fear was we never knew if he was actually reading the paper or glaring at us. We preferred to think he was glaring, which meant we dared not enter a room he was sitting in while reading.

In addition to filling us with unhealthy dread whenever he was around, my father was a violent man. I once went to school bleeding from my face after my father had whipped off his leather belt and beat me with it. When the other kids at school pointed to my face, I cried. The small holes from my father's thick belt stayed on my face for a little while. There were other incidents with my siblings, but I just said all that to say how alcohol had control over my father's life. I've since forgiven him but it sure took a long time.

You know, it's sad to see the amount of homeless people sleeping on bus stop and park benches with empty bottles and cans of beer on the ground beside them. This is a very common occurrence around the world, not just lovable old Seattle. Some neighborhoods here, like Pioneer Square, are just filled to the brim with nodding drunks scattered all over. Wouldn't it be nice if all of these alcoholics were really Hemingways-in-training? Seattle is already a pretty literate and creative society; I suppose a little more added to the mix wouldn't hurt. I'm sure all the homeless have an interesting story to tell, anyway. Maybe one day I'll walk around, interview the homeless and let them tell me their story so I could make a book of it.

Out here on the streets you see more sleeping bags than cars. Blankets of all shapes and sizes and thicknesses and colors abound. Some are old, some are new, some are borrowed, some are just stained with piss. There are several social service operations in place to help the homeless, but with every passing day, it seems like nothing more than an exercise in futility.

Homelessness and hopelessness go hand in hand, like caviar and Chardonnay, or Michael Jackson and a 12-year-old male visitor to Neverland Ranch. And with hopelessness comes the drive to numb that feeling of loss. Getting back up on your feet requires not only considerable strength but a reason to get up in the first place. Homeless alcoholism, really, all alcoholism, is nothing more than a slow suicide. The alcohol, then, is a double-edged sword – it numbs your pain while it slowly kills you.

Alcohol Abuse Disorder (AUD) and death by the bottle is prevalent in America. No age group, race, religion, gender, sexuality, social standing, nationality or creed is immune from it. Some treatment centers around the country are so full that you sometimes can't get a bed for a month or longer. Naturally, if you're suicidal, you're not going to wait an entire month for help. I wonder just how many people looking for beds die in that one long month of their wait; I won't be surprised if it's depressingly high.

Conspiracy theorists say "the government" wants certain people to be alcoholic; i.e., they don't sell high alcohol content drinks like Four Loko in tony neighborhoods but only in economically depressed ones where they also peddle huge 64 ounce jugs of Olde English. Of course, I haven't been to every store in every neighborhood, so I can't verify this. If that is true, then it's a sad commentary. Yes, people in bad neighborhoods can just say 'no' to alcohol, but that's as likely as having the Queen of England's Labrador teaching calculus to mentally challenged students. It is what it is. Alcoholism exists. People die from it every day. People crash their cars and get arrested because of it every day. People rob stores and break into 4 Runners every day because of it. Little kids get beaten up or neglected by their mothers and fathers every day because of it. It'd be the bomb if everyone in America simply regulated their drinking to just the weekends in Napa, but that ain't happening. Gov't programs like the National Institute On Alcohol Abuse & Alcoholism NIAAA - https://www.niaaa.nih.gov/ - stay abreast on current methodologies of treatment. It's a huge and costly one, but in the end, it'll be worth it.

***

This chapter had originally ended with that last bit about NIAAA; however, just having two lines on a whole page seems like a waste of space, so let's have fun with…misplaced modifiers! For those of you who were too busy keeping up with the Kardashians instead of paying attention to your teacher in English 101, a misplaced modifier is a word, phrase or clause that is improperly separated from the word it modifies. To wit: "I brought home a puppy to my sister named Prince."

Obviously, Prince is the puppy, but in the sentence above, it seems like my sister's name is Prince. The sentence should have been 'I brought home a puppy named Prince to my sister.'

***

"Captain, something's coming up from the deep! I just saw it on sonar.

"What is it?"

"Sonar? It's a device we use to detect motion underwater. Didn't they teach you that in the Academy?"

***

"Hey, Mike. This letter was in the mailbox but it's not mine."
"Then whose mailbox is it?"

***

"My guitarist friend is in town. I'm gonna ask him to play."
"Play what?"
[Stands up straight and salutes.] "Play, sir!"

CHAPTER 17

Cross-Eyed Mary, Island Girl *and* Roxanne

"You can spend the money on new housing for poor people and the homeless, or you can spend it on a football stadium or a golf course." Jello Biafra, singer and activist.

Streetwalking and homelessness go hand in hand, like drug abuse and store boosting, or runaways and suicide attempts. Gangs often step in where parental coverage has failed. Now that Mindy and Tommy are hooked on smack and are homeless, the commonest way for them to make money is to sell themselves on the strip. They will be busted several times over the course of one year, maybe overdose once or twice, raped more times than they'd care to remember, pick up STD's like a janitor picks up litter, and end up losing their minds in the process. They will not wear the scars on their backs, arms and legs proudly; those only serve to remind them how close they came to death…and it's never too late to go there.

Drugs have an incredible hold on the human psyche. It can change an angel into a devil, a pious beauty into a savage zombie. Over the years, I've had the pleasure of meeting and talking to a few…hookers. (I actually hate that word and other words for prostitution. It's very distasteful because it belittles and reduces these addicted people to nothing more than sex machines). In any case, the four stories below are not about homeless folks who sold themselves for the love of the trade; they're in the game simply as a means of survival. Naturally, I'm not using their real names to protect them from embarrassment and me from a lawsuit.

Shiny is a blond, blue-eyed beauty that, if you weren't paying close attention, you would think was Britney Spears. Standing at just 5'2" and weighing around 125lbs, soaking wet with bricks in her pocket, she is an explosive firecracker, a rocket always on the verge of flying into space. She ran away from home at 14 and has been on the street ever since. She claims she was abused at home but this was never substantiated. I first ran into her late at night during one of my drug runs in an upstate New York hood. She was the mule for a bagman with low slung pants and a FUBU sweatshirt from the projects of East New York. The dealer was reticent to sell to me because, and I've heard this a few times, I look like 5-0. Shiny insisted that she knew me from "around the way" so Mr. East New York gave her the nod to slip me a thirty, which she did. After that, I met her a few times and eventually became her friend. (On the streets, "friend" is a term best loosely defined because friends can often turn on each other as quickly as a politician changes his mind).

Shiny was as unpredictable as she was pretty. One minute, she'd be sweeter than strawberry dipped in honey. Seconds later, she could turn into that three-headed dog from the Harry Potter movies, snarling and gnashing her teeth like a rabies-infected mongrel. I'm no psychologist, but if I was to guess, I'd say she was bipolar. She had a personality some might classify as being "flighty", that is, topics don't stay in her mind for too long. Smack in the middle of talking about shoes she'd suddenly veer off into Who-Knows-Where Land and start yapping about, say, cabbies that rip off their customers. Unfortunately, our friendship didn't last too long, and was doomed from the start anyway, because of her overly aggressive nature.

One night, I was cruising around the block, up to no good as usual, when I saw her standing near a gas station. I drove over where she promptly opened the door and got in on the passenger side. I asked her what's going on. Out of the blue, she slapped me so hard I thought my eyes would fly out of their sockets. "Hey!" I yelled. "What's that for?" "Gimme your money!" she demanded. Shiny? Trying to jack me? "You must be crazy," I shouted, pushing her away from me. She attacked me again but I was able to subdue her and kick her out of the car.

Shiny had flipped. That night, her eyes were dark and distant, like she was possessed by Belial, leader of the Sons of Darkness. Her voice even sounded different; raspier, almost as if she coated her larynx with sandpaper. In the span of one year, she could easily be in jail five or six times, and usually for the same crimes – solicitation for the purpose of prostitution. With each incarceration, her behavior changed; worsened, really. She barely smiled anymore. Everything around her had to be done quickly, like she had to hurry up for a deployment to Kazakhstan. Her friends were disappearing left and right. When I finally left that town, the only thing I heard about her was that she'd caught a long bid for drug trafficking. Maybe she might learn a thing or two from that, if not, the streets are always out there, waiting to welcome her back.

Would you believe I was the father of a four-year-old girl for one day? Yep. Her mother, *Sallie*, had "loaned" or "given" her to me while she went out on a binge. Sallie wasn't too specific about her intention because, well, she had bigger fish to fry. To pass the time, I took Sallie Jr. to a plaza where several stores were. We went into a drug mart, and when we left, she showed me the lipstick and gum she'd boosted. I shook my head. Four years old and already starting off on the wrong track. It wasn't her fault, though. That pilfering behavior could only have been learned from one source, and that would be her mother.

Sallie was far more itinerant than Shiny. Whereas Shiny preferred to stay within a few miles of town, it wasn't beyond Sallie to hitch a ride to the sticks which were accessibly only by mule or saddled goat. Sallie's taste in drugs was all over the place, not limited to one or two like most folks. Consequently, her habit got so bad that she used to sit on the sidewalk looking completely lost, picking the scabs on her legs till rivulets of blood dripped down to her feet. I'd ask her if she wanted her daughter back but, without turning to look at me, would answer, "Not right now" just as a car rolled up for her to jump in. Through encouragement from her brother, Sallie did go to rehab a few times. Every time she came back, she looked good. The color was back in her cheeks. She fattened up a little and swore that she'd never go back out to the streets again. Famous last words. Last thing I heard was she'd shacked up with some redneck stranger in the sticks of Fleishman's with Sallie Jr. I do know that, to this day, Sallie Jr. is doing well. She even has a daughter, too, but as far as mama is concerned, I have yet to learn if she's doing okay or pushing up daisies.

One of the saddest females I'd even encountered in my life was a Latin beauty named *Esmeralda*. I first met her when I used to give "house" to a few Mexican gang members when I lived in Hollywood. In exchange for using my humble, albeit tiny, abode in a motel, they'd sail me off to lands far, far away. *"Es"* and I got along right away. She had seven children but they were all snatched by CPS. Originally from Phoenix, she came to L.A. because she was being abused and in fear of her life getting snuffed out like a candle. With no place to go, she tricked on Sunset and Hollywood Boulevards, Echo and MacArthur Parks, and several other neighborhoods like Culver City and Westlake. For protection, she went under the wings of 18 St., the Hollywood gang that also kept me company (whether I wanted them to or not).

Like other ladies of the night, *Es* wasn't always that easy to find. One day, she thought it was better if we hanged out in a Motel 6 instead of my place because it was being watched by LAPD. I asked her if she had money for the suite; she said no, but not to worry because she "knew somebody." Instead of walking into the front of Motel 6 like normal people, we sneaked around the back, climbed over a fence, ran up a fire escape and entered a room through a window which was already unlocked. Of course, I was nervous but she assured me everything was going to be okay. About ½ an hour later, there was a loud knocking on the door. It was the manager. Quickly, *Es* and I collected all our belongings, flew through the window, zoomed down the escape, leaped over the fence and dashed back to my place. *Es* didn't come in, though. She said there were a few things she had to do and would return later.

Around 9PM, Es and an over-tattooed gentilhombre from 18th St. came by my place. The young man simply sat in a corner baking like Julia Childs while *Es* sat on the floor. She asked me if I had a boombox (this was back in the day when boom boxes were popular). I produced a small, old-fashioned tape recorder and asked if that was okay. She took out a Sinead O'Connor cassette from her clutch and proceeded to play just one song from it, *"Nothin' Compares to You"*, over and over again for a total of seven times in a row. While the song played, she bawled like a baby. I said, "You know, if this song's troubling you so much, you shouldn't play it." She said no, it was okay, and kept on crying like she was trying to drain her body of every drop of water. It was really a bizarre sight – Tattooed Love Boy in this corner trapped in the rings of Saturn, the Queen of Motel 6 crouched on the floor crying like a church on Monday (thanks, New Radicals), and me sitting between the two looking as confused as Fred Flinstone on his first day at Spacely's Sprockets. I don't know where Es is these days but I could only hope she finally got it together. Too many of us simply end up on ice cold slabs in generic morgues across the country with nary a sympathizer to wave us goodbye. And life goes on. That's just how it is.

Bryce was one of the most unusual persons I've ever met; not unusual as in violently scary, just different. In talking about his past, he was very vague but I did learn a few things. He was a 19-year-old transplant from Lincoln, Rhode Island to Hollywood where I first met him in a public library. His mother was Vietnamese, his father was Polish and his middle and last names reflected this. He was relatively skinny, having to rely for food from youth shelters or whatever scraps he garnered from the men whose homes he visited. The first thing you noticed about Bryce was his hair; some would call it a mane, a crazy mane, all knotted, long and wild from being abandoned for years. His glasses didn't sit on his face correctly; he had to constantly push them up as they slipped down often. His multi-colored articles of clothing, all of which were a few sizes too large and in desperate need of repair, did match; that is, if he was trying out to be the poster boy for Schizophrenic's Digest. Usually, he wore lime green tights, maroon shorts, striped pink and blue knee-high socks, and black Converse Chuck Taylors that he'd painted red and gold.

Bryce had two loves – arcade video fighting games and Sailor Moon. It was through him that I was first introduced to anime with titles such as Slayers, Fist of the North Star, Ninja Scroll, Cowboy Bebop, Ranma 1/2 and many others. It was also through him that I first heard of cheat codes for arcade games. I didn't even know they existed. He spent a lot of time researching them on the web, writing down cryptic instructions such as 'hold Down+LK+MK until the end credits appear' as well as several others to play hidden tunes, gain special powers, unlimited health, and so on.

After knowing me for approximately two weeks, I moved Bryce into the room I rented at a crack motel in Hollywood. I had grown to trust him enough that I believed I could close my eyes to him, and I was right. He was pretty trustworthy. Unfortunately, the motel was a magnet for every bad element in town – gang members, prostitutes, dealers, thieves and robbers. A few of them I hanged out with, the rest I shunned for fear they'd slit my throat when my back was turned. In a way, Bryce was kind of like my boyfriend; 'kind of like' because, to make money, he turned tricks with different guys around town. There were two particular johns he knew who he could go to when he was down on his luck otherwise it'd usually be strangers from the street. Around that time, deep in the throes of my addiction, I didn't care if Bryce brought the johns home…as long as I got something out of it, like money. (I never said I was an angel, remember?) As is usually the case, one particular incident arose which brought Bryce and I back to reality, the reality that death is always just one flick away.

We had a Mexican friend named *Mar*. Mar was a fairly good looking chap with ties to the wrong people. He was a police officer in Mexico City but had to leave the country because the family of a man he killed came looking for him. Mar was one of our drug suppliers and confidants and introduced us to a lot of characters that's probably best not to mention. One night, around two in the morning, Mar came knocking on our door, but because we were so geeked out of our skulls, wouldn't let him in. He kept knocking and shouting to come in but our paranoia prevented us from opening the door. After a few minutes of cussing us out, he finally left and we went to sleep. Around 2PM that same day there was a knock on the door. When we opened it up, Mar came in. He was disheveled with blood streaking down his face from the top of his head. A knife with a blade that looked to be about 5" long was in his right hand. Immediately, my heart went from a normal 70bpm to that of a hummingbird's.

Mar said he was so enraged with us that he wanted to put us out of our misery, but because he considered us as his friend, he walked around in circles stabbing himself in the head to prevent him from turning us into sashimi. Bryce and I sat as silent as lambs just in case he suddenly changed him mind and started some brutal carnage. We explained our extreme drug-induced paranoia from last night, hoping to calm him down. It probably worked because I'm able to write this today. After he left, I made up my mind to get out of town that same day and decided not to tell Bryce or take him with me because I was now scared shitless and wanted nothing to do with anyone or anything in Hollywood.

I obtained a room in a motel in North Hollywood near the Burbank airport. Hopefully, I thought, no one would find me there. The motel, nested smack in the middle of Little Sinaloa, was a good place to remain underground. Since all of the stores and people in that area were Mexican, I learned quite a bit of Spanish in just the six months I was there. Had my first taste of menudo there, too, as well as other dishes like lengua al pastor and carne asada. Just before I had arrived at this new motel, it was obvious that Bryce was slipping deeper and deeper into his addiction. He'd be gone for days them return looking like a lost puppy and sleep for practically 24 hours. He gave me the feeling that, because of his extreme recklessness, he wouldn't make it to 20. I haven't seen him since the day I left Hollywood, but even till now, I wonder how he's doing. I guess I'll never know. I do thank him for introducing me to anime. And sex. I was a virgin up until I met him and I was 37 when I finally lost my cherry. I've never had sex again; that one time was it, one and done. Better than nothing, I guess. Thank you, Bryce. See you on the other side.

CHAPTER 18
How *to* Pass *the* Time Without Street Pharmaceuticals

[This chapter is dedicated to the three or four homeless people out there who don't abuse any substances.]

"I didn't mean to be a songwriter; I was just writing for fun, you have all day to do it. I was homeless so that's all I had to do." Jewel, singer/songwriter.

This is not going to be a comprehensive, try everything list. After all, like Queen asked, who wants to live forever? The majority of activities on here are free; some may cost a little money but it may be money well spent. Some activities may be impossible for some, especially for those with physical disabilities. It would, of course, be ridiculous to put "climb Mt. Rainier" on this bucket list. That's so over the top it's not even feasible. Not only do you have to have training, but also the money for the climbing equipment, all of which is beyond the scope of the average homeless person. Of course, if you're only homeless because you're filthy rich and just wanted to see how the other half lives, feel free to go ahead and sign up with the "Climb Mt. Rainier" club while you're cooking your food bank chicken on the spit down at the park.

Volunteering. As this subject was already explored in Chapter 13, there's no need to suggest anything here.

Visit A Museum. Do you like art? How about terra cotta sculptures or historical artifacts? Here in Seattle, as in other metropolises around the country, there are all kinds of museums that have free admission. For instance, the Klondike Gold Rush National Historical Park in Pioneer Square is one of them. It has lots of pictures and information of miners as well as the artifacts they used while digging for gold in the Yukon. It's pretty fascinating; shows the amazing amount of sweat and blood some people shed in trying to get rich while helping the country grow. Of course, not everyone struck gold; quite a small percentage, actually. But what else did a man have to do in 1890? TV wasn't invented yet and grandpa still had lots of stories of the good old days waiting to be told. The Frye Art Museum is also free, and since it's located on First Hill close to the soup kitchen in the St. James Cathedral on 9th Ave., it's a chance to kill two birds with one stone.

Of course, no one works for free. Wouldn't it be nice if you can go to a landlord and tell him you can't pay the rent because you work for free, and he says that's okay, you can still have the unit because you're cute? Unfortunately, life's not that way so most of the museums have to charge admission for their exhibits. What's nice about this is that in some cities, including Seattle, the museums are well aware there are people like yours truly who never seem to have two nickels to rub together. Enter: free days. There are many sites on the internet which list which museums have complimentary days, like http://freemuseumday.org/cities.html. They list which institutions are free on the first Thursday of every month as well as those that are free all year round. You'll notice that the Bellevue Arts Museum is free the first Friday of the month. That's good because everything is expensive in Bellevue, so being able to knock off the first Thursday and Friday in a row in museums is not a bad way to spend the time.

Go to A Public Library. This is the place I spend most of my time, whether it's the one here in Wallingford or any of the others scattered around the city. I believe all cities and towns in the U.S. have at least one library, and if they don't, shame on them. Of course, I say that now, but watch – in 20 years or so there may not be any more libraries anywhere because all information can be obtained the web. Remember 8-track tape or the Walkman? See, it can happen. Opening times for each institution differs so it's best to go online and research the ones near you. If you have no access to the internet, just stop someone on the street and ask them. By stop, I don't mean grabbing them by the shoulders. Just be courteous, but here's a little advice   don't waste your time trying to ask anyone anything if you haven't bathed for a while and you smell like downtown Pittsburgh; they will avoid you like TB.

Libraries are a thing of wonder these days. I remember the musky old ones I went to that used to carry vinyl records. I'd ask if you've ever seen vinyl, but since they've had a resurgence, the question is moot as, these days, hipsters and yuppies spend upwards of $100 on albums and thousands of dollars on vacuum tube sound systems their grandfathers used to buy for $60 or $70. The quality of the music on vinyl is still nowhere near that of a CD or DAT, but Gen Y's software engineer friends will be twice as impressed as if their hosts had provided audio entertainment on CD's alone. As a matter of fact, reel to reel recorders, cassette tapes and floppy disks are still in use, the reel to reel recorders and cassette tapes by budding recording engineers and floppy disks by the US nuclear force. True; you can't make up this stuff. But I digress.

The libraries in Seattle, especially the main one downtown, serves an important purpose – they provide a place for the homeless to hang out during the day because the shelters are closed at 6AM and won't open till 7PM or so. That's not to say you should check into a library for a little shut eye. Their security guard will wake you up with the quickness, so don't even bother trying. Anyway, there are so many things to read and do there that, if the printed word doesn't scare you, the time will just zip by without you even noticing. There's no way I can list everything these libraries contain; besides, the joy of discovery is part of the fun. Apart from the usual books, newspapers, magazines and DVD's, there are also internet computers, E-books, online reference sources, etc. It's interesting that, whenever I visit a library, most of the computers are already in use. Makes you wonder how many people are reading Dostoyevsky or watching cat vs. baby videos. My money's on porn; I can't be the only one in town with a dirty mind.

My main use for Seattle's public libraries is their powerful Wi-Fi. It's juicy as hell. Seriously, pop into one of those with your smartphone, table, laptop or what have you and you'll get a free connection that's as strong as 5G or T1, or whatever's in use by silicon giants these days. Streaming or downloading movies is smooth and effortless there, as is videoconferencing if you're into that. I'm glad the size of movies is smaller compared to their older cousins. What I mean is DVD video, at 4.2GB per film, doesn't look as good as, say, H.264. This format, whether AVI, MKV or MPEG, looks very good on computers and they're usually around 1.4GB per film. Even the new high definition H.265 movies clock in at around 1.5GB per film. Their 4K picture quality will probably be lost on a small monitor, but it'll look phenomenal on the spanking brand new 65-inch 2160p 4K UHD Smart Curved LED TV you'll buy as soon as you hit the lottery.

All is not perfect in Library Land, however. As of late, their bathrooms are attracting more and more drug users who occupy the stalls for 30 minutes or more. Some of the private rooms in the libraries are also being used by people to smoke weed. Not nice. It's bad enough that, a lot of times, you hear babies screaming while their mothers peruse the aisles or people talking loudly on their phones, but it can be downright upsetting when the man who just dragged himself in from the cold is reeking of cigarette smoke or weed and elects to sit next to you. Arrgghh!! And people wonder why I'm prone to strokes!

Go for a Walk. Even if you're in a wheelchair or scooter, this doesn't exclude you, just so you know. Walking is great exercise especially since it's free. Places to go walking abound everywhere, from public parks to lakes to school tracks (when they're not in use by the students) to public trails. Seattle's Burke-Gilman trail is well trod. It is 27 miles along and winds through many different neighborhoods. Sight-seeing on foot, wheels or inline skates. Can't beat that. I try to get in at least two miles a day especially since my body starts kinking up from sitting down in one spot with this computer. City streets are ideal for walking; lots to see there. Quiet, suburban streets? Not so much. Whenever I walk through those neighborhoods I can feel eyes on the back of my neck, like I'm casing the block or something. And I'm not being paranoid, either.

My old friend and I decided to walk 19 miles, from downtown Seattle to downtown Bellevue, via the I-90 Bridge which would also take us to Mercer Island and Factoria. We left around 8:30 AM and got to Mercer Island a few hours later. About 1/4 mile into Mercer Island, a police officer got out of his car and approached us. "Excuse me, gentlemen," he began, "did you see a black guy on a bicycle?" I replied, "Nope. The only black guy I've seen for miles is me." We also told him we take the occasional morning constitutionals and decided to visit Bellevue that day. He said okay then let us continue on our merry way. My walking partner, who is white, and I believed the cop wasn't looking for a black guy on a bicycle at all; he was just checking us out to make sure we weren't looking to burglarize any of the local resident's 4K LED TVs. How could a mobile cop with access to every nook and cranny not find a black guy on a bicycle in a milk white island neighborhood? We'd just walked the entire span of the I-90 Bridge, which was nearly two miles of Lake Washington boredom, then arrived on Mercer Island where, if you stood on top of any overpass or went overhead in a copter, you can spot a black guy on a bicycle for miles. That's like saying you can't spot the wolf in a field of sheep. Nice try, though.

Visit the Parks. In most cities, there are always cool parks to venture into. In Seattle, some of the more scenic parks are the Arboretum, Discovery Park, Volunteer Park, Green Lake, and Gasworks Park. Gasworks Park is interesting because there is a hill in which you can climb and see the entire Seattle skyline and Lake Union with possibly the best seat in town. It's also home to the old gigantic machinery that was used to power the city back in the day. A few vagrants also make their home among the preserved pipes in the park which, of course, the city frowns on since all city parks are not supposed to be utilized by the public from 11:30 PM to 4 AM. In any case, things being as the way they are at the moment, the increasing mass of homeless do have to sleep somewhere, park or no park.

Visit a zoo. Some zoos across the country have no admission charge. That's right. They're absolutely free to enter. Seattle's Woodland Park Zoo, unfortunately, is not one of them unless you're a toddler less than two years old. I didn't add aquariums to this list because their upkeep is expensive and they would have to recoup their money somewhere. You can always find out which zoos are free to enter just by googling it or visiting this site - http://www.trekaroo.com/list/free-zoos-across-the-us. Naturally, it'd help if you lived in the same city as the free zoos because, being homeless, you can't afford to travel too far or pay the parking fee, around $15, if you drive. Some of the free zoos include The National

Zoo in Washington, DC, the Saint Louis Zoo in Missouri, Lincoln Park Zoo in Chicago, Como Zoo in St. Paul, Minnesota, and so on. I've spent many a day in the Bronx Zoo with my old buddy, Dan. I must say, I do miss those times, but the satisfaction of watching nature's bounty in real life can't be experienced any other way.

See free live shows. Are you a fan of rock, jazz, hip-hop, blues, classical, funk, Klezmer or Andean pipe music? You're in luck. Most cities sponsor free concerts at different locations such as parks, downtown squares, restaurants, etc. They're usually listed in the entertainment section of the local Sunday paper which you can peruse at any library for free. And, of course, there are always those state fairs and city festivals, some of which have free admission. The local library should have more information about these free events as well as many others not mentioned in this book. Another way to listen to music for free is to stand just outside a bar or club that has a glass wall which allows you to see and hear everything. It'd be nice if there was a national directory of such places because admission prices can cost upwards from $5 or more. There was a club in downtown Providence with a glass wall so I did see a few free shows. One of them was Jewel when she was just starting out. There's also a bar in my neighborhood with a glass wall where you have direct line of sight to the stage. That's a ghetto way of listening to live music, but when you're dirt poor and homeless, what else choices do you have?

Feed the birds. This is actually more pleasurable, and calming, than it seems. If you've got crackers, bread, croissants and time, you could easily make a few new friends, albeit ones you can't talk to. I mean, you can talk to them, just don't think you can talk to another human being after that, though, because they'll think you're crazy, turn, and walk the other when they spot you coming down the street.

Birds have different personalities. If you go to a lake, you'll notice the coots and Canadian geese are the least timid. The coots skim right across the water with their blue feet to be fed if they recognize you from earlier times. Geese are also very brave; too brave, as a matter of fact. They will eat out of your hand even on the first day but they can get too ambitious and try to snatch all the bread that's in your hand. And it doesn't help that they hiss like snakes, too. That alone can make you nervous and want to avoid them.

Ducks and pigeons are about the same on the timidity scale. They're a little more cautious than geese, but once they recognize you, they won't feel so afraid. It is interesting that ducks and pigeons recognize faces. When the pigeons see me walking up the street they fly down off their roost and flap in the air around me to catch my attention. The ducks that recognize you will eat out of your hand but they won't be as aggressive as geese.

Crows are even more timid than pigeons and ducks. They do recognize faces but they're very apprehensive animals. No crow has ever eaten out of my hand; the closest they get to where I'm sitting is usually around 4 to 6 feet. When they do get some food, they stick around and eat it if you don't seem a threat or just fly away with it. Sea gulls are even more timid than crows. I'd say the closest they get to eat my tossed food is about 10 to 12 feet, maybe more. That's preferable anyway because gulls are way too loud to listen to up close. It's like they have shrill bellows for windpipes.

Crows are also very territorial birds. They'll descend upon you – not attack, just descend – to try to scare you away from their fledgling's nest. Walking through some neighborhoods you won't, of course, know which tree those jet black urban flyers built their home in; you will find out, however, the second Mama and Papa Crow come screeching and squawking loudly at you from above. How bold are crows? I once saw two of them giving a bald eagle grief high up in the sky. Every so often, they'd dive towards the eagle, hit him, and fly back a little. I watched this aerial show for nearly five minutes, the eagle circling around in the same area and the black crows trying to intimidate him. I was actually waiting to see if the eagle would say, "You know what? I'm tired of these damned crows," then suddenly attack and smite them with his mighty talons. I wonder what the eagle's thinking was. Bird of prey vs. scavenger – no contest. The eagle knows that. Maybe he was just having a little fun. Maybe, as soon as I stopped looking, he turned those two annoying pests into crow nuggets. Serves them right.

Sea gulls have an interesting personality. They show how they appreciate you by flying gracefully about 20 feet in the air above you, circling around, displaying their wings like models on a French runway. Their vision, like all birds of prey, are deadly accurate. The Northgate Mall gulls that know me prepare to greet me from the moment my familiar 2001 Kia Optima rolls up in the sprawling parking lot. As soon as I exit my trusty steel steed, a few of them, perched way up high on the nearby security lights, start squawking, or whatever that screeching noise they make is called. The squawking notifies other birds that "the feeder" has arrived and, within seconds, about 30 or 40 gulls come flying towards me like a scene from "The Birds." I do feel bad when I have nothing to give them, but when I do, boy, they sure make me feel like The Pied Piper, swarming around and picking up my delicious tidbits with the utmost of relish.

I've noticed there are two types of gulls here in Seattle: the normal white-winged ones with curved beaks, and slightly smaller light-tan ones with shorter, straight beaks. As a matter of fact, I'm not sure the light-tan birds are sea gulls at all, but as they say, birds of a feather. The noise the tan birds make are also different than the regular gulls. Whereas the white birds are extremely loud, the tan ones have a quieter, more genteel squawk. The tan birds, because they are a little smaller than the white ones, try their best not to get too far ahead in the pecking order lest they become brunch themselves. It's nice to be noticed and appreciated by the gulls. Just their simple approach alone is very welcoming, especially after a night of wrestling with my blanket in the freezing cold weather.

CHAPTER 19

The Truth About Cats *and* Dogs

"Seven out of ten Americans are one paycheck away from being homeless." Pras Michel, rapper/record producer/songwriter/actor.

Everybody loves pets, don't they? I know my grandfather did. He loved dogs – sautéed in mushroom sauce, stir fried with honey citrus glaze, poached with pears and walnuts, whatever was his fancy. Add a side dish of salt & pepper tabby and he's in 7th heaven. Seriously, though, pets are wonderful companions to have. They're loyal and will love you regardless of what you look like, where you live, how you smell, where you work, whether there's a thunderstorm, hurricane, earthquake, flood, tsunami, tornado, if you're deaf, dumb and blind and play a mean pinball, or what have you. Sadly, my heart breaks when I see and/or hear people yelling or abusing their pets. I know if I was your pet, and you treated me like that, I'd use every second of every day to try and get away from you as fast and as far as I can. And if you continued to beat me, but kept all the doors and windows locked, just remember you have to close your eyes some time. Then, it's on. You and me - mano a mano, baby.

Pets, especially, dogs, are deeply sensitive animals. They know when you're hurting, when you're happy, when you're concerned and when you're frightened. They're right there to protect you should Two-Finger Louie show up one day looking for the ten grand you owe him. If you have the patience of Job, you can even teach them how to bring you a brew from the fridge. Cats, on the other hand, are in their own little world. They're not your pets. Don't get it twisted. You can't boss these guys around. They own you. They view you as simply someone to service their personal needs – feed them, harbor them, pat them, let them rub their scent on you, then get out of their way. At least that's how my cat was anyway, and with razor blades for nails, I let her do whatever she wanted. I don't mind the sight of blood, just not my own.

A loyal, beautiful pet is great when you're homeless. Birds and reptiles are fine but they won't necessarily follow you around, protect you from the park ranger when he comes to evict you from sleeping in the shelter, or stop that pitbull racing towards you at 60mph from tearing you to ribbons. Cats can cling to you like glue but they have to be trained that way. There's an Asian guy I've seen around town who walks with his cat perched on his shoulders. Strange thing to see, but it does exist. I suppose any animal can be your friend…except monkeys. People try to do this all the time because, supposedly, monkeys are cute. I don't think so, but I'm not everybody. The problem with monkeys is, as soon as they become adolescents, say, seven years old, they suddenly turn on their owners, like they were pretending to be sweet these past seven years but just waiting for the right moment to rip master's face off with their hacksaw teeth. Monkeys make me nervous. I wouldn't even wait till they get to seven years. Seven days is long enough for me. Get that thing off my couch! Now!

By default, then, dogs remain man's best friend. They really come in handy on those cold nights when the one blanket you have just isn't cutting it. They're useful to have around when you just want to throw a Frisbee or stick in the park to pass the time. They're a good conversation starter, too. Chicks dig 'em.

"Ooh, what a cute pup! What's his name?"

"Sylvester."

"Sylvester? That's an odd name for a dog."

"I named him after my father."

"Oh, that's so sweet. Why don't you come back to my apartment and tell me all about your father?"

Okay, I made up that last hopeful bit about the sudden invite, but it can happen. You never know.

You'd think that I would be the last person championing for dogs, given my ardent fear of them. When I was a kid, maybe about five or six, I got my hands on a tricycle. Typically, I would've tried to take the bike apart to see what made it work (bad habit of mine), but I guess since I must not have had access to a wrench, I decided to ride it like normal people. Everything went smooth for the first minute or so; suddenly, a black dog came charging after me. Screaming, I pedaled as fast as I could to get away from the stray mongrel, but the mutt stayed on my tail like red on a rose. Then, as I turned a corner, I flipped off the bike. The noisy cur caught up to me, but surprisingly, didn't tear me apart. It didn't matter, though. The damage had been done. I was now traumatized for life. It's a strange thing. Even to this day, if I see a relatively large dog up ahead on the sidewalk, I will not hesitate to cross the street. I've even turned around and walk hundreds of extra feet to safely get to where I was headed. I wish I could turn that fear off but I guess it's stuck with me forever.

My fear of dogs is not the reason why I don't own one now. As a matter of fact, I probably should get a puppy, maybe something small like an American Eskimo or Scottish terrier, but just the thought of me bringing the pup to a park and having a German shepherd suddenly turn and attack it makes me queasy. From what I've noticed, dogs can be notoriously unpredictable. I've seen "non-vicious" dogs attack other dogs in parks out of the blue, and the surprised owner of the attacking animal starts yelling, "He's never done that before!" Yeah, first time for everything, sister. I don't know how it would work with me having a dog, though. I spend so many hours in the libraries that my furry little friend will probably poop in the car just for spite due to my constant absence. Anyway, besides my reticence, I still advocate for dog ownership for the homeless because they're great companions. End of story.

CHAPTER 20
Tell That Kid *to* Shut Up!

"I grew up with a family that had very little and were, at times, homeless." Misha Collins, actor.

"I want my children to have all the things I couldn't afford; then I want to move in with them." Phyllis Diller, comedian.

Kids. Don't have any. End of chapter.

Nah, I'm just playing. Kids are a wonder and a joy to behold. If they were silent till they turned 18, even better. (I think in one of my past lives I must've been the comedian, W.C. Fields. He was a hard drinker, a clown, a writer, a loner who used alcohol to induce fellow entertainers to socialize with him, an atheist who, nevertheless, studied theology, and couldn't stand children and dogs). Kids brighten our lives like celestial stars, entertaining us when the TV is on the fritz, and calling 911 when a sneaky burglar attempts a break in while we're passed out drunk on the living room sofa, spilled stout being absorbed by the spanking brand new marbled shag carpet installed just a week ago after having to pay the deposit for it in full because the carpet company would be going under in about a month and didn't plan to issue any refunds anyway. I, myself, don't have kids, but I'm guessing that since some people do, and I was once one, maybe I can shed a little light on what it feels like to be a kid growing up homeless. I'm not saying I had it terribly bad, after all, I'm still alive and writing this. But my heart does bleed for the innocent homeless kids who die like dogs on the streets to the tune of 13 per day in the U.S.

You see them everywhere, little Olivers, unkempt little kids, rummaging through the dumpsters in the back of department stores and fast food joints, sitting outside of supermarkets begging for change, or standing in a haggard soup line in the hot sun while their mothers smoke cheap unfiltered cigarettes nearby. At least there are mother & children shelters all around the country to serve their needs;

sometimes, though, the shelters are filled up, so mother and child end up in a crummy hotel, or worse, the street.

In some countries, homeless street kids can become notorious criminals and victims of a cruel state at the same time. Just check out the Brazilian movie Pixote or the Tunisian film Ali Zaoua: Prince of the Streets. These hapless kids and their friends steal wallets, peddle and abuse drugs, rob stores and people, prostitute themselves, burglarize homes and do just about anything an adult can do on the street to survive. It's a wonder any of these kids live to see adulthood at all. But through all that bleakness and desperation, some do survive, often turning back to help the new generation of kids hitting the streets every day. The situation is a little better in the U.S., though, as there are schools, welfare and drop-in centers everywhere, and places for medical care and so on. At least the world is on the right track, albeit slowly.

Being a kid on the street has got to be one of the most terrifying things a child can be exposed to. They don't know who to trust, who is simply helping them just to exploit them sexually, or who really has their best interests in mind. Kids are simply not physically or mentally strong enough to fight off kidnappers or, unfortunately, not fall victim to the pervasive lure of drugs and alcohol. I, myself, used to spend lots of time walking alone up and down the desolate, eroding beaches of Mayaro and Guayaguayare in southeastern Trinidad when I was a kid. It was safe back then. The beaches were always littered with fallen-off coconut tree branches, multi-colored shells and the carcasses of dead crabs. I think the worst thing that happened to me was when I was intrigued spotting a jellyfish, probably a Portuguese man-of-war, on the beach, knelt down to take a closer look and was stung by the little bugger on my right arm by one of its extremely long, thin tentacles. It hurt like the dickens, and bled, too. I'd thought the sucker was dead. I guess not. This happened over 40 years ago and the scar is still there. I learned quick and in a hurry not to approach those things again, let alone seek them out on the beach even if they seemed they were lifeless like my slimy little friend.*

In the greenbelts around Seattle you see entire families living in tents, their tiny little plastic homes erected on the grounds amongst the trees and bushes in makeshift neighborhoods they share with the local fauna of woodchucks, rats, beavers and raccoons. Some of the kids there do go to school; the city keeps statistics on these things so they are well aware they exist. Every so often, local charity organizations such as Union Gospel Mission (UGM) bring sandwiches, sundries and blankets out to the parks and woods where people stay, reminding the undomiciled souls that they have not been forgotten and help is always just a moment away.

StandUp for Kids runs several innovative programs, according to its website, that provides homeless youth the assistance, training and resources to make a successful re-integration into society. Some of the programs include Street Outreach, Drop-In Centers and Alternative Schools. Their services, as well as others across the country, can be contacted by a quick search on the internet or through addresses and numbers listed in phone books found in gas stations most everywhere. Here's StandUp's url: http://www.standupforkids.org/

Although I wasn't technically homeless as a kid in the sense that I didn't dumpster dive or sleep beneath banana leaves on the beach, I did come to the U.S. as an anorexic, near-broken 12-year-old. By then I had lived in seven places – Eastern Main Rd. in Sangre Grande, Ramnath Terrace in Sangre Grande, Brierley St. in Sangre Grande, a cousin's house in Port-Of-Spain, my grandmother's hut on Peter Hill in Mayaro, a house on Paul St. in Sangre Grande with my aunts and grandfather, then back to Peter Hill. If there were places before Eastern Main Rd., I don't remember them because my memory only goes back to when I was three or so.

I didn't see my mother from when I was 6 to 12 years old. She had fled from my abusive father to America and worked for 6 years to fly us up. Theirs was a troubled marriage, no doubt exacerbated by his frequent rum drunkenness and constant womanizing. My father, a man who basically grew up on the street, never worked, so my siblings and I were parceled out to different people, family members I presume. It was difficult to ascertain because it seemed every new woman was an aunt and every new man an uncle. Of course, as a kid, you took the constant moves in stride; it seemed as normal as falling asleep after a large Thanksgiving dinner.

My instability as a kid prepared me for my instability as an adult. The drive to move around a lot continued as I visited quite a few states, cities and towns in the U.S. and Canada, from Provincetown to L.A., from New York to Montreal, from Nashville to Seattle. It was worthwhile, too, because I did have quite a few experiences and saw a lot of things that I could never have garnered from a book. I could've done without the frequent come-ons at truck stops from Freight Driver Freddy and Chicken Hauler Chesney though, but that's another story. Besides, who were they trying to fool with those oversized belt buckles of theirs? Everyone knows they weren't packing nothing bigger than a pea shooter. Anyway, I think if I had explored the country with a kid in tow I would've just been preparing the kid for the same kind of unstable life I had. I don't know. There are people out there who grew up in far worse conditions than me and are doing just fine, children from war-torn countries, for example. My brother became a doctor. I was a nurse who also just happened to be an alcoholic and drug addict, but at least I did survive to tell this story. Having an unfortunate past, then, doesn't necessarily mean someone is doomed to failure. It just means they have a story worth sharing and an audience that's, hopefully, willing to listen.

***

*I've since learned that the Portuguese man-of-war is not a jellyfish after all. It's a siphonophore, an animal made up of a colony of organisms working together. This one comprises four polyps – a pneumatophore (the gas-filled float at the very top), the tentacles, the digestive organisms, and reproductive organisms. Fascinating, huh? A fist-sized modular home in the ocean that resembles a blob of Jello on steroids. The things you learn every day.

CHAPTER 21
Gimme Shelter

"When I was living in New York and didn't have a penny to my name, I would walk around the streets and occasionally I would see an alcove or something. And I'd think, that'll be good. That'll be a good spot for me when I'm homeless." Larry David, comedian, actor, writer, television producer.

I think, when you're homeless, you more or less develop a love-hate relationship with shelters. There are some you will thank your lucky stars for because they exist, and some you can't wait to spray an accelerant on and torch from the outside. Shelters are usually the first step you take when you're evicted; some of them are so bad, though, that you're better off sleeping on a park bench or an abandoned building somewhere. Horror stories abound about shelters. Would you like to hear a few?

Condescension. If there's anything I hate more than being insulted is being talked down to. Shelter workers are notorious for that. They figure they're in the position that you need them; you're at their mercy, so no sass, otherwise it's back to the sidewalk for you.

"Sir," you ask, "where's the bathroom?"

Shelter worker points down the hall. "What are you, blind?"

"Sir, can they turn the heat down? It's stifling in here?"

"If you don't like it then go sleep in the park!"

"Sir, my shoes are missing. I left them by my cot just for a minute to go to the bathroom and now they're gone."

"Oh well, that's your tough luck."

"Sir, do they have coffee here?"

"You must think you're in the Ritz-Carlton. Go to sleep!"

"Sir, the gentleman lying next to me might be dead."

"He probably is…about time, anyway."

"Sir, I think they're using drugs in the bathroom."

"Tell you what – you go call the cops, I'll go notify six o'clock news."

Fights. These are pretty commonplace in shelters. Flaco steps on Buddy's toes, it's on. Benny mistakes Julio for el hombre who impregnated his underage sister, it's on. Missy Mountaintop doesn't like the way Trailer Park Tracy is looking at her or her man, it's on. Cool G hates the fact that Lil Ton' just cut in front of the chow line like he owns the place, it's on. If you're lucky, you won't get caught in the crossfire and take a butter knife through your heart. Luckily, the police tend to respond to these common imbroglios rather quickly. This adds to the shelter's already bad reputation and its notoriety gets shot up a notch. Nothing to be proud of, of course, but what can you expect when a roomful of angry people get together? A song and dance that rivals those on Broadway? Keep dreaming.

Drugs. Even though every overnight refuge known to man has signs that say, "Drug Use Will Not Be Tolerated and Will Result in Immediate Termination from the Shelter," don't believe the hype. Shelters are a paramedic's wet dream. It's what pays for his kid's college tuition and the moorage for his 2012 Riviera Sport Yacht secured up in Shilshole Bay Marina. In the middle of the night, while you're trying to sleep in a room so stiflingly hot you can scramble eggs on the floor, the penetrating siren of an ambulance screeching to a halt will suddenly jar you awake. As you gather your senses and wipe the sleepers from your eyes, you notice Flaco is being hauled off to the nearest ER by a cadre of health professionals accompanied, of course, by the city's finest. Getting back to sleep will now be a tricky endeavor because the excitement has caused half the residents to wake up and their conversations about whatever Flaco did will occupy them till the first cock crows.

Safety. Some shelters, thankfully, go out of their way by using preventative measures to make sure people don't shank each other with sharpened toothbrushes in the middle of the night. Windows usually lack blinds because their cords can be used to strangle someone. Faucets lack handles because those could be sharpened into a carotid-cutting tool. I'd imagine getting gills from an angry shelter resident armed with a sharpened tap handle would be pretty gross.

Brooms and mops, thankfully, are usually locked up. You can't stab somebody with one, but you sure can make his bowels feel like they're about to explode from the inside out. Luckily, security guards are a common site in most shelters. They're usually not armed, just in case they suddenly get overpowered by a resident and all hell breaks loose, but some of them can behave like they're the Gestapo. Probably best to avoid these guys because, if you're asleep while they're wide awake, you're a sitting duck.

Diseases. I spent just one night in a cold weather shelter in L.A., just one night, but for a decade I had athlete's foot so bad I wanted to chew my toes off. Because the shelter felt like it was in the base of an active volcano, I took my shoes off to get a little comfortable. Interestingly, I only walked around the shelter like that for a couple of minutes but still picked up the athlete's foot bug somewhere. Thus, for the next ten years, I bought Tinactin spray after Tinactin spray. They did give relief but it was only temporary. The itching was so bad you can count the layers of skin I peeled off between my toes. Very aggravating. Athlete's foot is not so bad, though, when it comes to the bad boy himself – TB.

Tuberculosis, or consumption as it was called back in the day, was supposed to have gone the way of the dodo when polio snuck out the back door and into history. However, since history does repeat itself, there's TB again, waiting in the wings, or in this case, shelters, to infect a new group of people with its aggressive, blood-spitting bacteria. It's a good thing that TB drugs such as Rifampin and Isoniazid (INH) are still readily available otherwise a crisis the size of the Black Plague could ensue. Other diseases common to this population are HIV, Hepatitis B and Hepatitis C. Fortunately, many organizations are in the fight to treat and eradicate these and other communicable diseases. One such consortium is the National Health Care for the Homeless Council. Here's their website in case you need more information about their efforts and whatever else they do. https://www.nhchc.org/

Rats, roaches, bedbugs. *"Welcome back, my friends, to the show that never ends! We're so glad you can attend. Come inside! Come* inside!" (Thanks, ELP. R.I.P. Keith Emerson and Greg Lake). As a committed Jain, I will kill no animal, no matter how invasive the species, whether it be rats, roaches or bedbugs. I suppose that would make me the Worst. Roommate. Ever. That said, I won't stay at an overcrowded sanctuary that harbors them lest I be forced to crush one or two of those suckers with my heel. I do understand people's frustration with those little buggers; they used to bother me, too, once upon a time. But those miniscule critters are just trying to survive like everyone else, so who am I to deprive them of life, love and happiness? But I'm not everyone, so when it's time to call out the Orkin man, the city does just that – try to quell every infestation which registers a complaint high on the Richter scale. These creepy crawlies do bring diseases so you can't blame shelters for eradicating them, or trying their best to. Perhaps, in the future, scientists will find a way to prevent infestation in the first place, probably something along the lines of an ultrasonic device that should keep those impish creepy crawlies at bay. You never know.

Rape. Can you imagine being awoken in the middle of the night to some naked dude choking his chicken over you? It happens, and not just with men, either. Women have reported being harassed and sexually assaulted by security guards, shelter works, and other residents. That's a fact of life. You can't watch the baddies 24hrs a day. Some will slip under the radar and touch places they weren't supposed to; some may even go so far as to commit an act of fornication because their passed-out victim is too intoxicated to defend themselves. There was an allegation once made in NYC years ago that a gang rape took place at the Bellevue Men's Shelter on 30th Street. The victim was reportedly hog tied and raped by several residents and the security guard did nothing. An investigation by the authorities found nothing even though a few people insisted it really did happen. Rape, in addition to the physical trauma itself, yields long lasting effects such as PTSD, suicide attempts, drug and alcohol abuse, depression and anxiety. Society has been making great strides over the past few years to lessen its prevalence. It still exists, that means society still has some distance to go.

Clean & Sober. Okay, enough of the negative stuff. To be fair, some of these shelters, usually the transitional variation, are worth their weight in gold. Some really do maintain a clean and sober environment. They expect their residents to submit to a U/A at any time, see a psychologist and/or attend AA and NA sessions, sit in group meetings where they can talk about that sexually abusive uncle and negligent crackhead mother of theirs, and some may even have a curfew, all this in preparation for living a lifestyle that would make the pope proud. That's called tough love, and yes, some people, including yours truly, needed it sometimes. Speaking of the pope, there are a few shelters that are oriented around just that concept – religion.

Religious Shelters. I've stayed in two of these for a short while – one in Harlem and the other in Nashville. You're required to attend the Christian mass every Sunday and meet with a pastor or priest for one on-one sessions. If you're Muslim, Jain, Jewish, Zoroastrian, Buddhist, atheist or whatever that's too bad because you're still supposed to commit to pray to Jesus. To me that just seems like trampling on people's religious freedom in the sake of getting a bed. Their vain attempts to convert non-Christians fail miserably. Why do they even try? I guess it's in their charter and required by the archdiocese which pays their rent. Another problem with these shelters are, since they are faith based, chances are they look at the LGBTQ+ community as being an abomination unto the Lord and in need of salvation. Who started these shelters? My mother? She used to shove religion so far down my throat I'm surprised I'm not a cardinal by now. Faith-based institutions are sometimes notorious in their practice of discrimination. Some won't let you in if you're gay. Why? Because the Ultimate Authority told them so, that's why! I'm not surprised some people prefer sleeping in the street rather than having their will subjugated to the caprices of the religious few. That's no way to run a shelter, and that's no way to treat your fellow brothers in need. Dragging the destitute to an altar is just a poor attempt at forcing your religion on someone. Help them for real or stop pretending to.

Promising Signs. Cities like Seattle have a plethora of "famous" abandoned buildings. They're abandoned because their owners have long since died or moved on to other, more lucrative, projects; they're famous because they're supposed to be haunted. They've all been boarded up because their metal innards (pipes, radiators, etc) are a treasure trove for thieves.

This morning I went for a stroll around the boarded-up suite of buildings formerly known as the Naval Air Station Barracks at Magnuson Park in Sand Point, Seattle. The naval base, active from the 1930's to 1970's, was housed in the sprawling 350-acre park next to Lake Washington. When the base closed, the park could have easily turned into a giant homeless encampment and wholesale drug market; luckily, Seattle saw what could happen and stepped in right away to secure the area and eventually transform it into a safe, public-use space. Most of the park has been salvaged, and that's good.

One of the last remaining blights, however, is the boarded-up barracks. A few years ago, they were destined to become apartment units, but that plan fell through. I suspect it'll turn into a giant suite of condos in a few years as the area develops. Seattle, as a city, is growing so quickly that it's only a matter of years before some high-tech concern, like Amazon or Microsoft, purchase the buildings and turn them into work spaces and living units. That would be perfect for folks like me; it'd mean new places to beg for food.

CHAPTER 22
The Zen *of* Car Ownership

"Adversities such as being homeless and going to prison has made many people stronger." Philip Emeagwali, Nigerian inventor and scientist.

"If you own a home with wheels on it, and several cars without, you just might be a redneck." Jeff Foxworthy, comedian.

I was going to start off this chapter by pointing a finger at those folks who leave items in their cars because said items can entice burglars to smash through windows and grab whatever's there. Then I thought, "Nah, Robin. Don't do that. You're blaming the victim for being a victim." I wonder, though: do I have to scroll it via sky writing that people should never, ever leave things in their car that they want to keep? Almost every other morning when I wake up and walk to the nearest supermarket to wash my face, I see bits of broken tempered glass on the street right next to the vehicle it was in just a few hours before. Very common occurrence around here. Homelessness is on the rise, drug abuse is on the rise, it goes without saying that car prowls will also be on the upswing. It only takes one second for Crackhead Charlie to shatter a window, snatch that smartphone off the passenger seat, and bounce off into the sunset. Very often, the thieves don't even know what they're getting. Last week, this victim told me that some joker made off with his gym bag full of dirty sweats that he was meaning to wash. Jackpot, if the thief has an underwear fetish, otherwise it was just an exercise in futility. At least the victim could walk around the neighborhood and probably locate his dirty drawers dangling off a hedge somewhere.

Car windows are not cheap. If, like me, you only get $197 a month from Social Services, you can't afford to replace one. I can't even afford to get a speeding or parking ticket; all my money would be spent on fines instead of something more luxurious, like food. You have to be pretty diligent about keeping the burglars un-enticed. I wouldn't leave a newspaper on the seat because, for all I know, someone would still break in thinking the paper's concealing a Microsoft Surface Book, a Kindle, or some other electronic device. I wouldn't worry about small items like a can of soda or a pack of bubble gum. I definitely wouldn't leave a pack of cigarettes in plain sight, though. Cigs are a commodity on the street; it'll be a burning shame to spend $250 replacing a window because of the loss of an $8 pack of smokes. And, just walking around town, you'll notice that, obviously, a lot of drivers can't afford to replace their windows so they resort to the ghetto repair – plastic garbage bags and duct tape. That's a rather sad sight but it's as common here as the long beards on the Duck Commander crew.

Having a fully functioning car gives a homeless person an edge over those who are forced to share their meager sleeping space with rats and raccoons. One downside, however, is the cramped sleeping quarters. Many times I've woken up to find one or both of my knees are on fire. It usually takes me hours of walking around to finally ease the pain it took all night to create. But that's a minor caveat compared to the pluses car ownership gives. You don't have to bother with those rowdy, unpredictable buses loaded with feral teens. You always have shelter from the rain and protection from the cold. You don't have to lug around a 50-pound gunny sack with all your belongings and, if you're a man, you always have a private place to empty your bladder. I use a Gatorade bottle with a wide mouth; better that than risk getting arrested for urinating in public. It'd suck having to permanently register as a sex offender. Since they're pretty strict about that here, why chance it?

In the next chapter I talk about having to move your van every 72 hours because that is the maximum duration the law allows on a city street that has no restrictions. The same applies to cars. Every 72 hours, move that sucker at least 50 feet, to the next block if possible. Parking Enforcement Officer Paul hates the fact that he has to ride around in a cramped, tiny, three-wheeled Interceptor II which makes him look like he's just one rung up the ladder from mall cop. He'll be more than happy to write you a parking ticket at the 73-hour mark. His sergeant will pat him on the back for a job well done, the city will thank him for bringing them revenues, and the ticketed driver will gnash his teeth so loudly he'll start spitting out chunks of enamel whenever he speaks; PEO Paul can then go home and sleep in peace knowing that the world is a better place because he's in it. Oh, BTW, Parking Enforcement has at least 10 ways to know if you've went past the 72-hour mark; unfortunately, they're not allowed to tell the public what they are. I'm guessing that Peeping Polly with the brand new binoculars in the French Colonial up the block is one of them. Don't thing you're not being spied on. They didn't put up all those "Neighborhood Watch" signs because City Council was bored one day. Also, erasing the chalk mark Parking Enforcement left on your tire makes no difference because they can still tell if you'd moved your vehicle or not. That's what they told me anyway.

I once made the mistake of taking some anti-histamine medicine during an evening rainstorm. The combination of the pills and the rain made me super sleepy. So, instead of risking driving drowsily in the downpour, I figured I'd wait it out by resting in my car in the QFC parking lot for an hour or so. Sitting in the passenger seat, I fell asleep. When I awoke about one hour later there was a piece of paper underneath the left windshield wiper. I went to see what it was, probably an advertisement to get one free week of exercise from a new yuppie gym opening in town. Nope. I wasn't that lucky. It was a parking ticket for overstaying my 90-minute welcome in the lot. Really? I received a ticket while I'm in the car? First time for everything, I guess. Anyway, it took nearly two months, but I did get the ticket forgiven. The powers that be at the Imperial Parking Company were sympathetic to my homeless condition and gave me a break. Very nice of them. I can't complain. The ticket was for $72. There's no way I could afford that with my extreme lack of funds. Later on, when I make a fortune on Family Feud, I'll send the Imperial Parking Company a thank you note and a box of chocolates.

There are four words a homeless driver hates hearing the most – "You can't sleep here." Nothing's more annoying that being awakened by some power-hungry poseur tapping loudly on your window and ordering you to vamoose. Even though it happens a lot you could never get used to it. I don't think the human body was designed to be woken up suddenly like that. I won't be surprised if some people get themselves killed by carelessly waking a man in the midst of a violent nightmare. To me, when I see people sleeping, I tread lightly because you never know. They could go to bed a mogwai but wake up a gremlin. Not a pretty picture.

Shopping malls can be relatively practical…sometimes. Most of them, probably 99%, won't let you park in their lots overnight. I mean, technically, you can but just be prepared to find a ticket or two beneath one or both of your windshield wipers in the morning. What's worse than a ticket, of course, is that blooming orange sticker with the irremovable glue they stick to your driver side window as well as being booted. Here in Seattle it costs $145 to have a boot removed, plus there are administrative fees, possible towing and storage fees, and you still have to pay all those tickets acquired while illegally parked in the lot. Where malls come in handy is their "Mall Walker" programs. A lot of malls do that. They open their doors early in the morning, say, 6AM to 8AM or so, and allow people to just sit or walk around, use the bathrooms and access the Wi-Fi before the stores open at 10AM. Pretty cool beans. Just know there's no sleeping there, though. Mall Cop Marty is always on the prowl on his quiet little gyro mobile, or whatever those battery-operated stand-in scooters are called, looking for scofflaws.

Here's a bit of kind advice from your Friendly Neighborhood Homeless Mall Walker: don't window shop. It's bad enough that you have to sleep and use the bathrooms in public; it's just adding insult to injury when you stare at jewelry, suits, cellphones, massage chairs, mattresses, dresses or shoes you can't afford. Spare yourself the torture, and eventual depression, by keeping a strong focus on why you're in the mall that early in the morning in the first place: you've found a cool place to chill, albeit for a little while, anyway. And if you're single, try your best to keep your eyes off the happy couples walking around hand in hand. If it helps, pretend they're in the midst of a bitter divorce and are just keeping up appearances in public. It will do you no good to sigh and wish you were coupled off like they are. Some people get lucky later in life. Maybe you're one of them. Keep the hope alive.

It goes without saying that you should choose a nice safe place to park. A quiet, residential neighborhood loaded with plants and trees will do just fine. A noisy street where shady people stand around slinging dope is probably a bad idea. American cities are a mish-mash of all kinds of neighborhoods, from business districts to gated communities, from wooded hamlets to pock marked ghettoes, so choose wisely. I prefer an area which is fairly 'Leave It to Beaver'-ish but just a stone's throw away from the main drag – it'll be quiet where I sleep but the neighbors won't view me as an intruder because they're used to seeing the madness that doth exist on the central avenues. I'd probably sleep even more soundly and safely if I parked in a completely chic neighborhood like, say, Mercer Island, home of Microsoft strongman Paul Allen and tons of physicians, sports figures, and businessmen. But I wouldn't chance it. As soon as my back is turned – crash! – there goes my windshield. I should've kissed it goodbye. Mercer Police would just shake their heads and say, "Sorry, buddy. We have no leads and no witnesses." Sure, they don't. Me sleeping in my car on Mercer Island is as noticeable as a big yellow stain on a department store mattress. The locals would let me know, in some type of fashion, that my kind is not welcome, so it's better just to stick around in my old familiar hybrid spots.

Cars are also nice to have because they're generators on wheels. I did make the mistake of sleeping with the radio and heat on during a particularly cold night which emptied the battery, but once you learn things the hard way, chances are, you're not going to repeat them. The cigarette lighter in my car doesn't work. If it did I'd buy a 75w power inverter to plug in my laptop, my main source of entertainment. I do have a 600-amp Black & Decker battery jump starter with a USB port and cigarette lighter plug, but I just save its juice just in case my battery dies again. The original battery I had did die so I bought a used one for $20 from a Pick 'N Pull in Lynwood. My alternator was also fried so a friend from the last transitional shelter I was in replaced it with one he exorcised from a Junker from the same Pick 'N Pull. Altogether, the alternator and battery set me back about $100. I'd say that's better than the $700 quote I'd gotten from Sears or the $575 from the Kia dealership on Aurora. Maintaining a car can be burdensome and expensive headache, so it's better to keep it in good shape rather than having to resort to repairing it. Parts are costly; finding them can be time consuming, too. And when you're homeless, your time is precious but limited. Finding food and a place to rest your head takes precedence over all else. Fix the car now? Sorry, that'll have to wait until tomorrow after you get some much-needed shut eye.

Do you want to hear some bad news? Of course, you do. Recently, I went into freak mode when I found out that renewing my tabs would cost $160. What?! For those silly little plastic things to stick on my license plates? Yep. King County charges an $80 road fix fee on top of their other fees (poop removal fee, street lights replacement fee, sea wall reinforcement fee, fee-paper fee, etc). Other counties charge $40, but of course, since I happen to scrounge in one of the most expensive retail markets this side of Tokyo, I don't have a choice. I suppose I can just drive around with an expired tab, but I'm not in the mood right now to research how expensive the fine for having retired tabs cost. As a matter of fact, I will research it now since this is a sort of tell-all book. Just gimme a sec.

Okay. I found it. RCW 46.16A.030. Failure to make initial registration before operating a vehicle on the public highways of this state is a traffic infraction. A person committing this infraction must pay a fine of five hundred twenty-nine dollars. I don't know how they came up with that unusual $529 fee, but whatever. It is what it is. I'm sure that, in addition to giving you that fine, they could also impound your vehicle. Now, that would suck. Impound is too expensive to fool around with, and I should know…from experience. Sigh. Who said being homeless would be like walking in the park?

CHAPTER 23
Vans, RV's and the Zen of Nonconformity

"I just think if I can go from being a homeless kid with a dream of being in the biggest band in the world and making that happen, I can do a lot of other cool stuff, too." Nikki Sixx, Mötley Crüe, Sixx:A.M.

Recreational Vehicles have come a long way since America started taking to the road with them in 1910. The latest models sport amenities such as portable satellite TV antennas, HDTV's, washer/dryers, Bluetooth stereos, self-contained composting toilets, LED lighting, and so on. The list is as endless as the pockets are deep. The higher end models are quite expensive, threatening to set you back at around $100,000 or more. The idea I had when writing this book, however, eschews these high-end vehicles for the rusty, handyman special VW buses that Chris McCandless lived in after he sojourned to Alaska for his fatal trip. Anyone can live comfortably in an air-conditioned four bed camper stock full of Ben & Jerry's ice cream and crispy kale sticks. Try living in a bus with holes in the floorboard, leaks in the ceiling, rust in the radiator, cracks in the windshield, windows that won't open, doors that won't completely shut, seats that won't remain in place, rocker arms so noisy they knock grandma's teeth out of her mouth when you go over the bumps by an elementary school, malfunctioning windshield wipers, blown out taillights, tires with exposed metal threads, blown gaskets, oil pan leaks, you name it. Murphy's Law is in full effect when you hit the road in a Junker: whatever might go wrong will go wrong. That's as predictable as a foul in football.

So, what is a poor slob to do when he gets kicked to the curb and his only possessions are the clothes on his back and the 30-year-old van in his driveway? Break down like a wimp and ask for his life back. Seriously, though, that seldom works, and that's because the ones who kicked him to the curb lost their own humanity years ago. Begging for forgiveness is as futile as asking a dope fiend to brush his teeth during a binge. Ain't gonna happen. The only thing the newly homeless can do is take a deep breath, steel his nerves, and prepare for a life where his van must be moved every 72 hours or face a hefty fine. And he'd better hope his vehicle isn't over 80" long otherwise he wouldn't be able to park it legally on city streets.

Luckily, America is a great place for life in a van. There are RV parks in every state, from Alaska to Wyoming, where you can pull up, plug in, and enjoy the wilderness with your fellow adventurers, maybe even take a bath or two when the weather allows. Just stay clear of rust bucket RVs that emit a foul-smelling odor all hours of the day and night. That will be a meth lab on wheels, and the chances of it accidentally blowing sky high are 1000 to 1. Plus, when the FBI does a surprise raid at that mobile chemical plant at 2:30 in the morning, you don't want to get caught up in some kind of dragnet. Messy stuff, clearing your name. If you're homeless it means you can't afford Alan Dershowitz or any of the best lawyers in town, so just find yourself another spot to rest your head. Pierre and Marie Curie won't be coming out of their little lab to bail you out anytime soon, either, so be careful.

Apart from RV parks, some of which contain cafeterias, exercise and game rooms, a couple of churches from the Atlantic to the Pacific are opening their hearts, and their parking lots, to the itinerant traveler, allowing them to camp out overnight and usually for free. That's togetherness at work, and that makes for better community as far as I'm concerned. Of course, some campers will take the church's kindness for weakness and go ahead and introduce hookers and drugs to the mix. This is a sad commentary for how many people choose to live. You give them an inch and they take a mile. You really hate to police your fellow man, but sometimes you don't have a choice. Will people litter when you tell them not to? Of course, they will. Will people abuse hooch, anesthetics and patronize call girls in nooks they're not supposed to? Obviously. Will people start fires, smoke, gamble, blast music and piss on plants and other items with impunity? Mankind is nothing if not predictable, and that's too bad because all it takes is one bad apple to spoil the whole bunch, girl.

These days, the amount of people living in their cars and vans is increasing steadily. Recent head counts across the country prove this to be a fact. Apartment and housing costs are rising faster than dough in a convection oven. There are bound to be casualties from the rapid, uncontrolled growth of the tech giants. Who can guarantee their job will exist tomorrow? All you can do is go to work quietly, keep your head low, do as you are told, don't raise your voice above a whisper to your superiors, and make sure those Pepto-Bismol tablets are right where you can quickly grab them just in case blood from that crater-sized ulcer growing in your stomach suddenly starts seeping through your nostrils. And if it just so happens that corporate life is much more unbearable than you'd like, don't head to the highest bridge for a flying leap. Invest in a small van and start life all over.

The key to surviving in a van is to make sure it's equipped and well maintained. That probably goes without saying, but it's often surprising to hear how some people forget to do simple things like buy tags, check oil levels, rotate tires, seal water tanks, inspect the air filter or replace the windshield wipers. You'd hate to suddenly find yourself in the midst of a hurricane because you'd forgotten to patch that hole in the roof this morning. Also, make sure the outside of your van is clean and in good shape, too. Mischievous kids have a knack for making mincemeat of the worst vehicles they can find. Why? They figure the owner doesn't care about it, so why should they? What's one more scratch? One more broken window? One more flat tire? The little brats don't care about the cost of their mischief. They'll actually blame you for forcing them to decimate your one and only abode. Still, try not to get enraged enough to install compound jets that spit flames from beneath your van. You couldn't afford the funeral costs for the little tramps or the lengthy prison time you'll garner.

Vans come in very handy when you've been walking around all day looking for food or a friend or just something to do. There's nothing like retiring to your nondescript house on wheels, jumping into bed, and dreaming of that great big castle in the sky which, unfortunately, will never come to fruition. Just remember to move your vehicle every three days. The general rule is that you must move your van at least 50 feet away from where it was last parked. That means simply driving it to the other side of the street won't work. Just to be on the safe side, leave it on an adjacent block. You can argue with a traffic cop till you're blue in the face, but everyone knows they're always right and you're always wrong, so why bother? Humble yourself and move your little fortress often. Those parking tickets do add up, and if you factor in the cost of gas, insurance, road fees, and the like, you'll soon find your wallet getting lighter and lighter while your nerves get thinner and thinner.

Vans also have one important advantage over lowly cars – you can have sex in them. Sure, you can do the nasty in a car, but your positions are severely limited by the tight space and the fact that Neighborhood Nelly can see what you're up to through your windows. When I used to drive a taxi, there were two separate occasions where women "went to work" on their men. Both incidents happened at night in the backseat and, believe it or not, both men asked permission to be pleasured like that. I agreed, not because I'm a twisted sex fiend anyway, but I'm an experience freak. Engage in oral sex with me sitting right there? Sure. If you're that brave, go for it. Can I make a video of it and throw it on the internet? That's what I want to know! Seriously, though, I think if my taxi was a full-sized van, both parties would've gone full horizontal. They were probably drunk enough to do it, not to mention I was being paid for a free sex show. You know, just before Mayor Giuliani shut down all the porno booths around 42nd St. in NYC, you would've had to pay $20 or more for a short viewing in one of those sticky rooms. Here, I was being paid to see a sex show. How cool is that?

The cons of living in a van are the lack of laundry and bathroom facilities, lack of a microwave, and the fact that some home owners would rather not have a van parked in front of their house day and night. Cars are more nondescript because they're smaller; vans just scream for attention. You also spend more money for gas with vans as well as paying higher tolls on some routes and higher taxes because of engine size and emissions. If it so happens that you don't have a portable toilet in your van, rest assured, there will be a few available where ever you may roam. Some, however, are not open 24 hours so you'll have to plan accordingly.

A neat, tidy, well-maintained, well-equipped van is one way to go if you're planning an alternate lifestyle away from rents, heating costs, mortgages, homeowners' insurance, school fees, light bills and landlord-induced headaches. Lots of folks do it and probably more will join in this mobile lifestyle as years go on and the cost of living keeps increasing. It's not so bad, really. Just find yourself a safe neighborhood, make a few friends, and enjoy the rest of whatever years you have left. Visit online sites like Coleman or Cabela's for ideas about water purifiers, portable electric generators, camping supplies, coolers, bedding, etc. They'll steer you in the right direction.

CHAPTER 24
National Parks

"Life is now a war zone, and as such, the number of people considered disposable has grown exponentially, and this includes low income whites, poor minorities, immigrants, the unemployed, the homeless, and a range of people who are viewed as a liability to capital and its endless predatory quest for power and profits." Henry Giroux, scholar and cultural critic.

New York City can kill you. Seriously, it can bury you alive with an avalanche of concrete and steel if you're not careful. Danger lurks everywhere you turn. Just riding the subways, staring at the endless walls of graffiti through their vandalized plastic windows, makes you thirsty for a quieter, calmer, safer place to hang your hat. Nothing puts your heart in your throat faster than stepping off the train on to the Atlantic Avenue platform in East New York where the flash of gunfire can be seen and heard from the restless, drug-addled streets below.

I'd be a hypocrite if I said I despised the inner city, after all, I was dependent on them to supply me with yayo. And they did, up to the gills. Just one subway ride from the safe confines of my rented hotel or motel room in Manhattan to Brownsville or Harlem could yield me a pocketful of goodies that, in essence, could've given me years in Riker's Island if I'd been caught. I was lucky. Oh, there were a few times I thought my heart was going to explode out of my chest from the unnecessary panic and nervousness I felt, and those were the times I said to myself, "Okay. This is it. No more of this shit. Get out now while you're still alive." But did I ever listen to me? Well, I did, for a minute or two. Once I started fiending for another hit, though, my fear would inexplicably disappear. Stop using now? Um, maybe tomorrow.

You know what sucks? Tomorrow never comes when you're trying to quit your bad habits. Anyone who ever says to themselves they're going to stop next week or two weeks from now or on their birthday or whenever is deluding themselves. Seriously. Addiction doesn't work that way. You don't plan to quit. You just do. Talk is cheap. The brain wants what it wants and it will do anything possible to make sure you keep flooding it with dopamine. So, what do you do to put the madness behind you? The more common ways are enter rehab, get help from family and friends, or distance yourself from people, places and things. Another is to pack everything in panniers on your broken-down bike and head for the hills. I was so frustrated with going around in circles that I had no choice but break free or die. Cue: National Parks.

America is a great place to live – if you can get there in one piece. I'm just joking. You've got to have a concrete heart if you don't feel sorry for the poor bastards around the world who live in squalor with no food to eat or medicine for whatever ails them. If these unlucky souls could eat the shotgun shells littering their gravelly, blood-soaked streets, they'd grow up to be healthy, strong, well respected citizens of their particular countries. But the reality is many of them won't grow up at all. Many are going to die virgins. Many are going to die hungry virgins. Many are going to die homeless, hungry virgins. Most are going to die hopeless, homeless, hungry virgins. And that's why I don't take National Parks for granted. They're actually life savers.

In most American states, if not all of them, you can camp out in the same spot in a National Park for 72 hours. That's beneficial especially if you have a bum leg and lack the fortitude to keep moving your tent and sleeping bag around like a nomad. Parks are pretty cool. Some of them have fish-stocked lakes, some have clear, delicious running streams, and some have splendiferous waterfalls. I tell you, once you've drank cold, fresh, mountain filtered water you'll never look at normal drinking water the same way again.

Living in the wilderness requires unbelievable strength and focus. It's not a simple matter of showing up near a lake one day with a basket full of bread, a gallon of light beer and a glassine of indica. Preparations have to be made. Did you bring a phone? Doesn't matter. You won't be able to reach anyone anyway because you're miles away from the nearest connection. Matches? Hopefully you remembered all those twig-lighting Boy Scout tricks you learned as a child. Bow and arrow? Unless you're Robin Hood, forget about that.

You stand a better chance getting into Hillary's knickers than impaling a rabbit with one of those. Reading material? That'll only come in handy when you run out of wood for the fire, unless you can stand reading 'Into the Wild' forty times or more.

There are many threats to someone living a solitary life deep in a National Park. Who'll get their back if a vicious gang of racists or anti-government types suddenly invade their living space? Criminals often hide in the woods and nature does absolutely nothing to lessen their evil ways. Cornering an escaped convict in a Park is as dangerous as stealing a tiger cub from its mother. Your best bet, then, would be to visit sites that are known to be safe or get a regular cadre of campers. You can visit the National Park Service's website for more information. I've linked to it here for your convenience. https://www.nps.gov/findapark/index.htm

Seriously, though, danger notwithstanding, one of the biggest threats to living such a quiet, non-social life is the risk of death from boredom. If you're schizophrenic, then you're in luck – you'll never be alone and will always have someone to talk to. If you're not, and you can't speak to the animals like Dr. Doolittle, then you'd better get used to silence fast because you're in for a heap of it. You'll wake up in silence. You'll piss in silence. You'll eat, drink, fish and hunt in silence. You'll chop wood, dig potty holes, swim and store wood in silence. And you'll sleep in silence. Just that one thought alone keeps most people from living in the woods. Sleeping in silence. For some people, sleeping alone and jumping off a skyscraper without a parachute is the same thing. Human beings, for the most part, are social animals, and there is a stigma attached to those who do go it alone, like they're crazy or they got something to hide like Ted Kaczynski, the Unabomber. Yet, it has been done for millennia, and it's not so difficult once you have the tools.

The internet has tons of sites that can prepare anyone for a life of solitude. All you have to do is Google "survivalist" or "prepper" and you'll be inundated with information from how to start fires to purifying water to heating water to baiting hooks to finding natural cold and pain remedies in the wild to identifying edible and poisonous plants to organic farming to Patriotism to the best National Parks for free camping to making rafts, log cabins and waterproof tents to creating an effective camouflage for yourself to hammock building. The list is endless. This site I've linked to is called *OFFGRID Survival*. It contains a huge list of survival websites and blogs as well as info about pertinent current and national issues. http://offgridsurvival.com/

Going it alone in a National Park requires nerves of steel, but it is common knowledge that the closer mankind gets back to his roots, the more relaxed he becomes. Recent brain imaging and studies have even noticed that. Here's the link to the site to which I'm referring. http://iheartintelligence.com/2015/10/11/great-for-your-brain/

Yeah, people will think you're crazy for trying it, but forget the naysayers. Remember, no one would be in America today except for the natives if Christopher Columbus had listened to all the kooks who said he'd sail off the edge of the world because it's flat. Now who're the crazy ones?

CHAPTER 25
National Perks

"Many foster children have had difficulty making the transition to independent living. Several are homeless, become single parents, commit crimes, or live in poverty. They are also frequent targets of crime." Charles Bass, Member of the U.S. House of Representatives.

Are there any benefits to being homeless, like, free places to eat or crash? Free housing or health care? More than a handful of idealistic teens think so. When mom and pop become too commanding, controlling and interfering in their lives they decide it's time to change, and that's okay. Maybe the separation will help both parties see eye to eye, sometimes not. So, the kids just pack everything up in used military duffel bags, grab their s.o., kiss the little sister goodbye and hit the long, wide, unforgiving open road without looking back. Adventure awaits, though they may not exactly care for it. Next stop: No Man's Land.

Homeless teens can take comfort in the fact there are shelters and hostels in every state. That's the good news. The bad is it's probably better to sleep in a giant hive of wasps than some of these shelters. Seriously, you wouldn't send your worst enemy to stay in them unless you really, really hated them. The hostels, designated mainly for young students, are much better because they're safer and well protected. A young 'un can just drop in, get information and maybe even a bite to eat before continuing on their way. Prices are usually pretty low there, and since you share rooms, at least you'll have company.

As it turns out, there are honest people out there who don't mind letting weary world travelers, even adults, sleep a night or two on their porch. Their numbers may not be legion but they do exist. I'm speaking from experience in regards to the lovely couple in Woodstock that "adopted" me for one night. No, they didn't molest me while I was asleep on their porch or secretly drain my blood for their satanic rites. Chances are they are sojourners themselves so they understand what travelers go through and, in that sense, were more than happy to lend a hand. I'll bet they've probably even doled out hot toddies of cocoa with those tiny marshmallows on top to strangers. I wouldn't be surprised. Obviously, you can't expect much hospitality if you look ultra-scary, like the lead singer from the Norwegian black metal band Blood Corpse. The white-painted face, black lips, black bats' wings around both eyes, blood-stained shoulder length hair, spiked collar, and jet black, chain-covered Edward Scissorhands getup, is scary enough without adding that glowing skull and crossbones thingy dangling from your nasal septum.

If you look hard and carefully enough you will meet nice, kind and friendly people to help you along the way. Some may even go so far as to let you use their shower should you happen to smell like Liquid Ass. Never heard of it? It's a prank spray in a bottle; the liquid is obtained from the butt cracks of meth heads that have been dead for at least two months. Seriously though, these nice folks don't mind the occasional rare company at all. Some will feed you, give you a beer or two, maybe even let you spend the night with whichever one of their sheep you choose. Okay, that's sick, but they say I always go too far, and I guess they're right.

You know, if you don't mind exposing yourself to every STD known to man, then you're in luck. Most homeless chicks I know are not particularly picky about who they see. Some are missing chunks of teeth, but don't let deter you. Nobody's perfect. The nice thing about homeless girls is, after a date, you don't have to go through the trouble of sneaking into their bedroom window. Some of these ladies are available for a good long while too while their baby daddies are finishing up their 15 to 25-year bid for manslaughter, grand theft auto and possession with intent to distribute. Some men take advantage of these love-seeking women, impregnate them then disappear the second a baby bump appears. It's not fair but that's how the world is. It's just a game and those who play the best hands collect the most dough.

There's a certain camaraderie amongst the homeless, like foxhole brothers or a deployment troop, and they are more than happy to share their weed with you. Now that Mary Jane is legal in quite a few of these United States, it's becoming more and more probable that you'll catch a contact high just walking down Main Street. Of course, should you get lucky and come into some herb yourself, don't forget to share it with your fellow down and out brethren, after all, they did come through for you in your time of need. Being greedy may cost you your tent or sleeping bag while you're asleep so learn to share, homeboy.

You can't beat the extra time you suddenly get by being homeless. Since there is no rent, mortgage, moorage, lot fees or land taxes hanging over your head, you are now free to pursue your lifelong dream of being the blues guitarist that can finally give Eric Clapton a run for his money. Or you can catch up on that much-needed shuteye you've been meaning to get for decades. I know someone who now spends most of his days playing GTA V and other XBOX games instead of filing in the congested line of the rat race. Another guy I know plays Diablo III nonstop. I suppose they're making up for time lost chasing the normal things in life, like a job, house, marriage and kids. Does that make them bad people that their lives are less stressful than Corporate Man's whose ass gets handed to him on a daily basis by customers on the phone or bosses who could care less that he's one opiate away from a nervous breakdown? Sometimes a man just has to stop, take a long, hard, deep look at what his life means then come to a decision that could possibly alter the trajectory of his existence forever. Not an easy choice to make. Some will succeed; some will fail. But, like Yoda said, "There is no try. There is only do."

One truth you'll encounter from the homeless is the rarity of political correctness within their ranks. Yeah, I know, just because they live on the street doesn't mean they have to talk like Tourette's on overdrive. However, it is what it is – the honesty can be liberating as well as damaging at the same time. I actually would rather know straight up if someone is racist so I won't waste my time trying to converse with them. Also, just for the record, let me say that I don't condone racist behavior or language; in fact, I despise and condemn it. That said, some of the homeless can be pretty raw. At any given moment, you'll hear things coming out of their mouths such as, "What does she see in that retard?" or "Who's that cracker looking at?" or "That nigger stole my shit!" There is absolutely no filtering of language in this population; no grammar Nazis to put them back in line, either. From my experience, if you just so happen to end up among a crew of people who make George Carlin sound like Mary Magdalene, don't sweat it. If you ask them to turn the coarseness down a notch, they will. That's not guaranteed but you never know.

You ever been to a husband calling contest? What about buckin' the bronco at the Cactus Canteen in Campbellsville, Kentucky? Cow tipping in Mesa, Arizona? That's why I like rednecks. Political correctness requires a bit of intelligence to cover up the bullshit you really want to say, a gift that is lacking in the Appalachian living, tobacco chewing, moonshine drinking, incest loving, no teeth having, backwoods loving, 2nd Amendment worshipping redneck community. Them moonshine boys say what they mean and mean what they say. Ain't no fakery in that bunch and that's absolutely fine by me. So, they don't decorate their words to sound like a Hallmark card, that's okay. In an urban office, yes, you do have to come across like Martha Stewart on Colace because, these days, you can get fired just for looking at someone the wrong way. Out in the street, though, you have no paychecks rolling in; you don't have to stutter in your process of choosing the right words to say. Freedom is yours to enjoy. So, go ahead. Cuss like you ain't got no sense. Just don't tell nobody I encouraged it. I got enough trouble as it is, capeche?

CHAPTER 26
Obama, Phone Home

"Actors look at life in a different way. When I meet people, I know that one day I may portray that person or someone like them. It may be a cop or a homeless guy. It helps to pay more attention to people. Everyone I meet, I retain something from them, something from their personality. It helps me to portray realism in my work."
Mekhi Phifer, actor.

Even though the free government phones program didn't begin with Obama (it began in 2008 during the presidency of George W. Bush), it took off during his term and appropriated the moniker Obama Phone. Obama Phones, in case you were hiding in a foxhole in Beirut for the last ten years, is a free cell phone, usually with a limit of 250 minutes/month that is distributed to the economically challenged. You can add more minutes but it'll cost you some loot. The original Obama phones were simple flip phones that also allowed you to send text messages. The newer ones are smartphones which you can use to surf the internet. Again, your data usage is limited, so if you want more time you'll have to sell more than Real Change newspapers for that.

As is the norm for American ingenuity, some companies that distributed the phones found a way to acquire more dead presidents by scamming social service organizations. I know, the horror, right? People who already owned phones, including Obama phones, were using fake DSHS ID numbers to get more phones. Both the recipient of the new unit and the distributor were rewarded and Uncle Sam was none the wiser. Eventually, the government caught up with the scammers and now makes it more difficult to get more than one phone. Of course, when there's a will, someone will find a way to circumvent the new system.

I'm old school so I have one of those nostalgic flip phones that resemble a Star Trek communicator. Unfortunately, it doesn't get internet. That's okay because I have this computer and I can always access the web at the mall, the libraries, or different supermarkets and stores around the city. Comcast/Xfinity also has millions of hotspots so it's relatively easy to tap into the internet just sitting on a bench in the street somewhere. The connections are usually not that strong, but something is better than nothing, so I can't complain.

I may go ahead and join the revolution by getting a smartphone; then, like everyone else, I can stand waiting for my ride at the bus stop, deeply immersed in videos of babies vs. kittens, while grandma gets mugged of her social security check by one of America's Most Wanted right across the street in plain sight. Unbelievable. How smartphone addicts cross the street without paying attention to traffic and still not get hit by a crosstown bus is beyond me. With my luck, I'd fall in a manhole while watching Peter Gabriel's "Sledgehammer" video. On second thoughts, maybe I'll stick with my Obama Phone. Less drama that way.

Elsewhere in this book, I talk about how important it is to take your hard-earned valuables out of your car when you dock it in a parking lot or somewhere on the street. It's like the prowlers have radar for this stuff. Yeah, it's inconvenient, but necessary. Of course, needless to say, make sure you lock its doors, especially at night. I was once awakened by someone jiggling my handle at 3:15AM. As soon as I sat up he rode off on his pint-sized bike. Maybe I should have left my Obama phone in plain sight. He probably felt sorry for me and was trying to break in to give me a modern cell phone. Too late to find out now.

***

Every so often I come across statements on the internet such as, "90% of the homeless are on the street because they choose to be. The other 10% are out there because of misfortune." It'd be nice if that was true, but it's not. It's similar to when people say, "Why do you want to be gay? If you get the right girl you'll be okay, you'll see." I've met a lot of homeless people over the years. I know that journalists writing articles on homelessness sometimes pretend to be street dwellers because they want to see what it feels like first hand. Can you imagine, though, having to wake up every few minutes because you don't know if that rustling sound you hear is just grandma walking her Pekingese or some pranksters getting ready to set your sleeping bag on fire? The absolute saddest video you could ever see on the internet was posted by the Dnepropetrovsk maniacs from Ukraine. It's gruesome. It's unbelievable violence against the homeless. I saw it already so just take my word for it. I only expose myself to carnage like that because seeing is believing. A lot more people have deep, mental issues than authorities realize. I wish it were a simple matter of pulling up your boot straps and heading to the assembly line at the factory. That would be nice.

ADDENDUM 1

When I first wrote this book, Obama was the President of these United States. Now, it's Donald James Trump, business mogul from New York City. As of this writing, the whole Obama phone/Obamacare situation is in limbo. Will these benefits stand the test of time? Will they really build a 2,400-mile-long wall along the Mexican-American border? Will Tom Brady, the winningest quarterback in NFL history, go on to become the next POTUS? It could happen. Look at Dwight D. "Ike" Eisenhower. He was the general during WWII. So popular was he that he eventually became the 34th POTUS. I'm not going to take any cheap shots at Brother Trump at this time because, as yet, I don't know where he stands on homelessness. So far, most of his executive orders have been focused on constitutional law, big business dealings, and so on. Nothing yet about the little man. It remains to be seen what he thinks of us small fries.

ADDENDUM 2

In December, 2016, the FCC changed the rules on Obamaphone ownership. If you accidentally drop your smartphone in a parking lot in the middle of the night after grocery shopping, and a car runs over it, you have to wait two months before any Lifeline carrier will issue you a new phone. (Yeah, I learned this the hard way).

CHAPTER 27
Shock Me, Baby

"I wasn't going to have enough money to pay for a Good Lifestyle, which meant I'd feel ashamed, which meant I'd get depressed, and that was the big one because I knew what that did to me: it made it so I wouldn't get out of bed, which led to the ultimate thing - homelessness. If you can't get out of bed for long enough, people come and take your bed away." Ned Vizzini, It's Kind of a Funny Story.

"...And God saw all that He did was good, then said, "Let there be electricity...except where Robin wants it to be." The Seattle Bible, revised edition.

Why cities don't implant electrical outlets in trees or rocks is a mystery to me. Don't they realize the solar powered hotpot doesn't exist yet? I guess that's my fault for being so nomadic. In my past life, I may have been a wildebeest on the Serengeti, always in search of arable land, fresh running water, and protection from the hyenas and leopards that keep me in their crosshairs day and night. I wouldn't have had all that trouble if I was given the skin of an armadillo, but such is life. You can't have it all.

The quest for electricity is actually a fun one; to me, anyway. I once stayed in Lincoln Park in Providence, temporarily breaking away from society like I was a member of the Chris McCandless Adventurers Club. Summer had just begun; the nip in the air I'd just left behind in New York was gone, replaced by the effluvient serenity of the New England sun. The powers that be in Providence saw fit to install several lampposts scattered throughout the park, albeit with the caveat that no AC or DC outlets be available for public use. Believe me, I looked. It was like trying to locate the center of the universe; I gave up after half a day of turning over every rock, branch and twig I could find. The only thing left to do then was – gasp! – camp without it. I did have a traveling companion at the time, so at least unbearable loneliness wouldn't threaten to tear my soul apart. By the way, naïve me truly believed that Lincoln Park was unique in its lack of outlets. I couldn't have been more wrong.

I faced the issue in other places I spent time in, like Griffith Park in Los Feliz, a relatively quiet section of LA just northeast of Hollywood. The only electronic item I owned that needed a regular charging was my cellphone but Griffith was not going to accommodate that little request. That's okay, though. The park was mainly used for sleeping in my car during the day; at night, I stayed in the West Hollywood Library parking lot. For some reason, I thought West Hollywood would've been safer because, well, everybody knows gay folks aren't violent, right? As it turned out, West Hollywood was no safer than any gay neighborhood sandwiched in an urban landscape such as the East Village in NYC, The Castro District in San Francisco, or Capitol Hill right here in sunny Seattle. It's the out of town, small-minded riff raff who swarm into these enclaves and raise royal hell.

I really don't fault cities for keeping the electricity off in parks that do have outlets. In Cal Anderson Park on Capitol Hill, when the power was on, people used to plug in their refrigerators. The city thought that was overkill because the juice was only to be used for simple devices like cellphones or rechargeable flashlights. And just in case anyone got more bright ideas, just for good measure, the city went ahead and cut all the power to all the shelters in all the parks. No electricity, no camping. They will turn it on, however, for special events like weddings and concerts. What happens though if, like me, you have a hotpot and don't want to eat cold cans of beans and peas and boring granola bars every day? You scout for power, that's what.

So far, I've found about three areas of the city where I can plug in my hotpot and laptop in peace. No law enforcement officer or security dude has bothered me about it, but maybe that's another one of my "yets." In other news, some ingenious inventors have been coming up with all kinds of solar powered ovens. These are basically boxes with sun reflectors built in so that the interior of the oven could heat up to about 350 degrees, good enough for frying eggs or nuking that vegetable casserole Aunt Bibby made for you yesterday. I can just imagine how long it'd take to warm up her delicious dish. By the time it's ready, you would've been asleep for three hours already. Of course, since you're also dependent on the sun to be out for a relatively long time, you'd have to plan well in a perpetually overcast city like, say, Seattle, Portland or London. In other words, don't lock those granola bars away in the lockers at the county gym just yet.

I went hi tech about six months ago. The portable emergency Black & Decker car battery charger I bought has two outlets, one for 12v DC like a cigarette lighter, and the other, a 5v USB port for charging small electronic stuff. I've used the unit to jump start my car already but haven't utilized the ports yet because the plugs in both my laptop and hotpot are the 120v AC two prong variety. I'm sure I can use an intermediary component like a 75w power inverter but I don't have the money at this time. Maybe I'll get lucky and find one in the street. It can happen. Strange thing - I have a history of finding things I need such as a water cooler with cups on it when I was thirsty, gloves when my hands were freezing, hats when my head was cold, pants, shirts, shoes, sweaters, food when I was starving, car wax, etc. I haven't used the wax yet, mainly because I only remembered about it just now. Tomorrow's Saturday. Maybe I'll shine my car then.

Did you know they made solar powered generators? The one I saw is about the size of a 30w tube amp and, since it doesn't use gas, you can use it inside; no fumes, you see. If I put it on a Radio Flyer I can drag it around town, kinda like having a dog with no legs. (You don't walk it, you drag it, you see). Now all I have to do is find $40 for that little red Flyer wagon and $2200 for the generator. It can be done with the bullion I get from DSHS. All I have to do is give up eating for a year and it'll be all systems go. Geez. I can feel my ribs protruding from my chest already. At least I'll get back that boyish figure I used to have when I was in high school.

Update: This morning I went around looking for a place to plug in my electric clippers to cut my hair. The power outlet in the men's room of the Northgate public library was kaput so I walked next door to the community center. Would you believe that ALL the external outlets in the center had been covered up my immovable metal plates?! Some nerve. So where is an undomiciled gentleman such as myself supposed to plug in his hot pot, cell phone and computer? I finally went and used the men's room at the Red Robin across the street at the mall, but I had to give myself the one minute haircut special just in case the manager happened to walk in on this half naked writer. I'm telling you, Seattle is becoming more and more anti-homeless every day. Right now, as we speak, 65 new buildings are going up in and around the Emerald City. There are so many cranes across the skyline the area resembles a giant Sim City. I've been keeping my eyes on the news to see if any of those buildings will be utilized as affordable housing. The latest thing I heard was that Paul Allen (Microsoft, Portland Trailblazers, Seattle Seahawks, etc) was going to donate $1M to build one of those newfangled steel modular buildings already in use in Europe. $1M seems like a piddly amount but I guess you take what you can get.

Update 2: I notice they've been making strides in handy, portable, light-weight solar-powered generators lately. The ones I've seen deliver about 3W to 200W, and that should make them powerful enough to recharge smartphones and other small electronics. The others I've seen which supply 300W or more and can power laptops but will set you back about $1000 or more, too expensive for the average homeless person. The smaller units cost around $80 to $200. China seems to be at the forefront in this type of technology, but I wonder how useful their machines are? Solar cells take a notoriously long time to recharge a cell. I can just imagine how long I'd have to leave my unit out in the sun before 1. My battery gets recharged or 2. Someone runs off with it. Since Seattle is not known for ample sunlight, perhaps purchasing one to use here is a moot point. Never mind.

CHAPTER 28
Homelessness Advocacy

"You call this progress, because you have motor cars and telephones and flying machines and a thousand potions to make you feel better? And people sleeping on the streets?" Howard Zinn, Marx In Soho: A Play on History.

"We must accept finite disappointment, but never lose infinite hope." Martin Luther King, Jr., civil rights activist.

There are many ways to petition for the rights of the homeless, from registering in an anti-hunger coalition to attending seminars where local politicos appear to answer questions about bills and key proposals being presented to congress and legislatures. Advocacy, then, takes many shapes and forms, from low-level street interviews and head counts to bipartisan referendums at the state level. Each one is effective in their own way, but there is no magic fix-it wand, nothing that can be waved over a sea of despondent souls that'll instantly house them. How can the homeless help in advocating for themselves?

There are several alliances created to tackle this ever-growing problem: King County Coalition on Homelessness, National Alliance to End Homelessness, Homeless Rights Advocacy Project, Disabled Homeless Advocacy Project, Washington Coalition for Homeless Youth Advocacy, National Coalition for Homeless Veterans, Housing and Homelessness Advocacy Day, and many others, all of which can be located via the internet. Karen Murphy posted an article back in 2009 on Causecast.org which explained 10 ways to advocate for my disenfranchised brethren and sistren. All points are as relevant today as they were a few years ago.

Know the issues. In other words, learn basic facts on why people become homeless in the first place, including veterans who, in all fairness, should be living the life of Riley after watching heads being shot off in Iraq, Afghanistan, Pakistan, Syria and elsewhere.

Connect with a local coalition. Karen believes there is power in numbers and you can contact the National Coalition for the Homeless for guidance in reaching your own local advocacy group. She promises they exist in every state.

Find out what advocates are doing in other cities. She mentioned three specific people - Eric Sheptock who keeps a Facebook page and advocates for Washington, D.C., Cathy ten Broeke, the coordinator to End Homelessness for Hennepin County in Minneapolis, and Randle Loeb, a Denver advocate with bipolar and who, himself, is homeless. Cathy and Randle also currently use Facebook as of this writing.

Create a plan. This is where you enlist the aid of your local coalition after you've spent time talking to the homeless and their service providers.

Engage your local elected officials. I think I used the wrong approach when I wrote to Mayor Ed Murray two months ago about his plan to bring in an outside consultant to the tune of $70,000 for 9 months of work. I don't know. I really hate being skeptical, but because the price of rents keep going up, as well as gas, food and everything else, and the sheer numbers of homeless are increasing steadily, I just thought that the $70K would have had better use elsewhere. In any case, don't be forceful like I was because it brought no results. Instead, Karen suggests you testify at local planning and budget hearings, attend neighborhood and public speaking places to voice your views, solicit the support of local care providers, the faith community, and civic and veterans' groups, and follow up with continuing correspondence and personal meetings with the local decision makers.

Personally meet with your legislator. (I know...advocating is hard work, right?) She suggested you stay focused, don't be antagonistic, and realize the personal touch is crucial to getting your voice heard.

Involve the media. I don't have a cousin at Fox or ABC News, but if you do, superb. If not, you'd have to resort to calling them or writing letters like us common folk. And by writing letters, I mean email, not snail mail. Are post offices still even open? Local newspapers and magazines can also be contacted, too. Again, keep your letters warm, cordial and friendly. If there is even a hint of vitriol in your language you can be sure they'll right click-delete your note in no time flat.

Get involved with a local street newspaper. Here in Seattle it's called Real Change and people sell them in front of supermarkets, drug stores and busy intersections for $2. That's kind of steep but it is for a worthy cause. Their main office is easy to reach and they can give you tips about employment and other issues related to homelessness.

Register people experiencing homelessness to vote. According to Karen, you don't need to have a home to take part in this political affair. You can contact Michael Stoops at (202) 462-4822 or mstoops@nationalhomeless.org to obtain the voting rights registration manual and poster.

Encourage advocacy where it counts. Here she suggests you take advantage of high-participant affairs like Thanksgiving dinners where you can provide papers and pens for folks to write to their legislators, have a "Call in day" where you offer cell phones at shelters or soup kitchens for the homeless to call their legislators, or "Reverse Panhandle" where you get the homeless to hand out quarters and ask people to call their legislators. That last tidbit is a little tricky. I'm not sure I'd give a roll of quarters to my homeless brothers to distribute on the street. Sorry, but I know my people well. You give them a roll of quarters and they'll be in the wine shoppe so fast they'll make Speedy Gonzalez look like Droopy, at least the ones I hang out with anyway.

CHAPTER 29
Rights *of* the Homeless

"Happiness lives in every corner of your home, and if you are homeless, it leaves under the leaves of trees, hiding beneath the sky's cloudiness. All you need to do is to find it with patience." Munia Khan, Beyond the Vernal Mind.

"To deny people their human rights is to challenge their very humanity." Nelson Mandela, South African anti-apartheid revolutionary, politician and philanthropist who served as President of South Africa, 1994-1999.

What is it about the human species that, with our intelligence, prosperity and fortitude, we sometimes forget that we are not alone on Planet Earth? We are all connected and dependent on each other, much like the ocean which depends upon its existence from the presence of the land beneath it. I've always been interested in human rights; maybe that's probably a byproduct of having PTSD, I don't know. Years ago, I created a Peace Board. It's a framed collection of pictures of eight civil rights leaders I admire – Aung San Suu Kyi from Myanmar, Martin Luther King, Jr., Nelson Mandela, Mahatma Gandhi, Mother Teresa, Cesar Chavez, Tenzin Gyatso – the 14th Dalai Lama, and John Lennon. (He wrote *"Give Peace a Chance"* so he counts). A photo of my 15-year-old Peace Board can be seen on my blog, The Writings of an American Author. https://seattlewordsmith.wordpress.com/

You have the right to be treated with dignity. Just because you're as poor as church mice doesn't mean you have to be treated like their droppings.

You have the right to medical care. You shouldn't have to walk around with a festering sore the size of a grapefruit on your buttock because you're being denied antibiotics, and you shouldn't have to rely on Homeless Harry to drain the green juice out of that sore by the light of the full moon with his rusty 25-year-old military-issued knife.

You have the right to be as creative as possible when you fly your cardboard signs as you spánge out on the I-5 off-ramp. For instance, if you're trying to raise funds for that once in a lifetime trip to Kiev, advertise that. If you're trying to buy enough Lego blocks to build a replica of the White House in a deserted field in Arlington, feel free to broadcast that, too.

You have the right to refuse to shower – forever. However, if citizens give you wide berth when you walk down the street to avoid getting stung by the horse flies and biting midges circling your carcass, don't get pissed. Citizens have rights, too.

You have the right to neglect your dental hygiene. Feel free to believe that the toothpaste industry is just a North Korean conspiracy to take over the world; just don't go crying to the dentist when your molars start dropping like F-bombs.

You have the right to dumpster dive at Captain D's; however, don't you dare walk to the restaurant's front counter and tell the clerk you can't eat those fish sticks you found because the maggots have built a home in them. Instead, just dispense yourself a little container of ketchup and cover the maggots with it. You won't know the difference and neither will your friends.

You have the right to tote your belongings around in a shopping cart. You don't have the right, however, to tell K-Mart or Target to "stuff it" when they come by with a pickup truck looking to get their property back.

You have the right to walk around naked in the street. This also gives you the right to yell bloody murder when the C.O.'s at County Jail start hosing you down with water so cold your gonads recede up into your chest because, as you know, it'll be about one week before you can retract those hairy twins.

You have the right to refuse to go to a shelter. When the outreach workers come and pester you about it, just tell them you'd rather get your nuts caught in a shredder than spend the night at one of their flea-infested hostels.

You have the right to mental health care, and so does your invisible friend who no one believes exist except your schizophrenic cousin from Long Beach who smoked so much dope that he never leaves his motel room because he thinks there are snipers in every tree in the city.

You have the right to sleep on Mr. Harrison's porch in the middle of the night, but if he suddenly decides to take his 4-year-old, 200lb Rottweiler out for a walk at 2AM, unleashed, don't blame me for what happens next.

You have the right to argue, threaten, push and shove each other on the street, just don't expect the police to intervene because, being homeless, you develop an uncanny ability to call the cops during shift change, and since it takes one hour for them to suit up, one hour to be briefed, and one hour to get their coffee and donuts from the Starbuck's across town, you're S.O.L.

You have the right to not be forcefully crippled and enslaved into begging like some of the poor children in downtown New Delhi. Furthermore, you have the right to not have your eyes gouged out with hot spoons or your legs amputated to serve the slavers of Mumbai or the rest of the world.

You have the right to reject bread or cantaloupes from the food banks if they're moldy unless, of course, you're creating penicillin antibiotics to combat grandma's yeast infection or the bacterial cellulitis on your son's left foot.

You have the right to not be taken advantage of when you're cross-faded (high and drunk at the same time). You also have the right to file a complaint with the local police department in cases of harassment and not have them dismiss you as being just a messed-up troll.

You have the right to reject the hateful vitriol of ignorant people who see the homeless as being able-bodied abusers of social services and government assistance. Perhaps they'd prefer it if the mentally ill among us wore signs around our necks announcing our ADHD, schizophrenia or bipolar, with symptoms so far off the Richter scale that holding down a job is difficult. But, since we do have a right to our privacy, scarlet letters are optional at this time.

You have the right to follow in the footsteps of your Great Depression-era hobo ancestors by taking to the rails in boxcars, whether they are insulated, non-insulated or refrigerated, and seeing America in all her glorious splendor.

You have the right to hitchhike from town to town so long as you don't hurt anyone, make anyone uncomfortable, steal from anyone, or hit on your driver's little sister. Just so you know, according to Wikipedia, hitchhiking is legal in 44 of the 50 state (I didn't know that; I thought it was illegal nationally), and you should not stand in the roadway or hinder the normal flow of traffic.

You have the right to a reasonable expectation of privacy. No, this doesn't mean it's okay to shoot half a vial of Propofol into your ankle in the bathroom at JC Penney's or do the nasty between the dumpsters in the back of Pep Boys with that tramp you just picked up from Aurora Ave. It means you should be able to catch some winks while you're stretched out in your Coleman tent even if it is located just 10 feet from U.S. Route 44 in Connecticut or Massachusetts.

You have the right to access hygiene facilities 24 hours a day. Gone are the days of Seattle's shiny, silvery $900,000 free-standing restrooms. They were being occupied mostly by prostitutes and addicts anyway. Hospital ER bathrooms are open 24hrs. Just use them for their intended purpose, because if you get busted for alternative use, don't ask me to bail you out from County. I'm broke.

CHAPTER 30
The Homeless Ten Commandments

"Homelessness is not the result of not having a house, it's the lack of a soul in a body." Goitsemang Mvula, writer and thinker.

I suppose you thought Moses was the only one who had rules etched in stone. What would any self-respecting book on hoboism be if it lacked divine inspiration? I didn't come up with these commandments, by the way. I saw them in a fortune cookie in Chinatown. Scouts honor.

Thou shalt not patronize the same food bank twice in the same week. You can try but since you have to register at most banks, and show your ID when you come in, they do keep a record of your visits. And don't think you can get over on the volunteers just because they're pushing 90. They're still as sharp as they were when JFK was the president.

Thou shalt not covet thy neighbor's cardboard box. That's just rude; he didn't go scouring through the waste in the back of the mall for nothing. Anyway, it wouldn't kill you to just amble politely into a department store or grocery outlet and ask for a big box. They'd be more than happy to help out their fellow less-fortunate humans. Furniture stores also throw them away frequently as does the occasional restaurant, so you might want to check those out, too.

Thou shalt not beg for change in thy neighbor's space outside the Jack in the Box. How would you like it if, one day, with your empty stomach growling from unbelievable hunger, you walked over to your spot near Subway but someone's already panhandling there? Chances are, if you're really weak from ravenousness, you wouldn't even have the strength to wrestle a moth, so why tempt fate? Plus, pilfering someone else's space is just asking for a knockdown, drag out, no holds barred fight. Who needs that?

Remember to honor thy food stamps and not trade them for cash. Back in the old days, when food stamps were distributed in booklets, people used to fence them at their local crooked merchant for beer, cigarettes, gas or cash. I knew some guys who used their food stamps to gain entrance to $13 spots (brothels). It'd cost them about $40 in food stamps but at least they'd be able to get their whistle wet by a poor Colombian woman smuggled into America on pretenses she was going to be working at Tavern on the Green in Manhattan.

Thou shalt arise when the early birds do. If you sleep out in your car like me, you don't have a choice. The black crows around here are so loud you can hear them for blocks. Add their shrill "awks" to the atonal melodies of singing March wrens, black-headed grosbeaks, dark eyed juncos or whatever else exotic birds flitter around here in the Pacific Northwest, and the early morning, 3.30AM, cacophony will drive you insane.

Thou shalt not urinate in the hedgerow near the public library. Seriously; the stray cats already do it, so you don't need to add to the stalwart scents already emanating from that burning bush. Plus, if the librarians see you stooping in the hedge, they *will* call the lavatory police who are on speed dial, in case you wanted to know.

Thou shalt shower at least once a month. (Probably the commandment I break the most). What is a poor bloke to do when he lives in a car? Sure, I can drive up to the free showers at Green Lake every day, but since I don't own my own oil well, I can't afford it. However, on scout's honor, I will shower more often if I smelled like a whale that's been beached for two months. Then again, maybe I do smell funky but people are too polite to tell me. Let's put it this way. If I walk past a bouquet of gardenias and they wilted and died on the spot, I'll head to the showers, okay?

Thou shalt not keep thy belongings in an old shopping cart with loud, rattling wheels. All carts are not created equal. The ones you find in grocery stores are fairly noisy because they're overworked like a gold miner's mule and are constructed from cheap rubber and poorly forged metal. When I'm trying to catch some Z's in my car I can hear Broke Foot Benny with his Shop Rite cart coming down the block. No wonder he's toothless. All that vibrating would knock my teeth out, too. By contrast, Target's carts are a joy. The soft silicone wheels are quiet and the metal monkey-basket barely rattles. Someone pushing a cart like that could sneak up behind you and steal the tin of Red Man from your back pocket without you even noticing.

Thou shalt not visit the same dumpster twice in one night. Yep. Don't be greedy. There are many mouths to feed in any city on any given night. Share the love. Are you going to eat those hamburgers with the fruit flies crawling all over them? Probably not. What about that expired salad in the bag? You don't even like kale or arugula or have any idea what the balsamic garlic vinaigrette packed in with it is. That expired Hawaiian pizza you found in the back of Domino's should be able to feed you and a few of your friends, or you may even be able to save some slices for later. Cold pizza isn't so bad once you get used to it. And you can always use the crust for a door stop if necessary.

Thou shalt not sleep nude on the bench outside the K-Mart. Yeah, the Retail Police frown on such ruthless behavior. Same thing if you're butt naked in front of Taco Bell or the little Mexican food truck across the street from Washington High School. If nudity's your thing, then wait for the summer solstice parade in the middle of June in the more progressive cities across America. That's when you can really let your freak flag fly. Paint yourself to look like the Orion constellation or the Japanese flag; no one will say a word. You can even ride in the parade on a borrowed bike with Mr. Johnson waving hi to everybody. That's your one and only chance to show off, otherwise it's County where Cousin Bubba's waiting for you.

Thou shalt not usurp thy neighbor's number at the food bank or seat at the dining table in the hot meal kitchen. These crimes against humanity are punishable by reciting ten Hail Marys and begging for forgiveness.

CHAPTER 31
Just Give Us What We Need

"The first time I was homeless was when I went to Atlanta. I was in a homeless shelter, then when I got a job I used to miss the curfew for the shelter. So I ended up sleeping outside in the streets." Jay Electronica, hip hop recording artist and record producer.

Ever heard of the reggae band Black Uhuru? I don't listen to them that much these days like I did in the past when I was soaked knee-high in similar artists like Steel Pulse, Barrington Levy, Bob Marley & the Wailers and Third World, but they still remain one of my favorites. They have a song which has been going through my head for decades called *"Solidarity."*

"Everybody wants the same thing, don't they? Everybody wants a happy end –
They wanna see the game on Saturday / They wanna be somebody's friend –
Everybody wanna work for a living / Everybody wants their children warm –
Everybody wants to be forgiven / They want a shelter from the storm –
Look at me, I ain't your enemy / We walk on common ground –
We don't need to fight each other / What we need, what we need –
Solidarity."

Which, of course, brings us to this chapter lovingly called 'Just Give Us What We Need, We'll Take Care of the Rest.' Yeah, we can use a little solidarity, just throw it in the homeless gift basket along with these other wishes:

Affordable Housing. This is pretty self-explanatory. As the tech giants grow larger and larger, and the land becomes more expensive and gentrified, the poor are continually squeezed out of the homes they've lived in for years then cast to the wayside like banana peels. Condos, completely equipped with gyms, saunas, steam rooms and hot tubs, are popping up everywhere. Right now, I receive in one year what it costs to rent a modern studio apt. for ½ a month. I'm not complaining. Poverty has its rewards, but my personal choice is a difficult one and not for everybody. Apodments, tiny one room apartments, are being built as we speak. They're perfect for students and single workers. But they are still expensive, clocking in at around $900/month for each unit. Tiny bite-sized cottages are also being built around the country, so that's an alternative. They'll usually set you back about $6,000 or more but there's no mortgage or rent because you'll own it. You'll just have to pay lot fees as well as electricity, water and waste fees.

It'll be interesting to see if America adopts dense-housing alternatives already being used in Spain, England, Japan and Hong Kong. In Spain, they convert abandoned malls and defunct businesses into identical 2 & 3 bedroom units, creating upwards of 7,000 apartments in one small area. England has communal housing, that is, everyone who lives on the farm is responsible for its upkeep, from watering plants to harvesting fruit, from milking cows to tending sheep. There, no one rides for free. And then there's super creative East Asia with their skinny apartments which, in all actuality, resemble elevators with windows. If it's privacy you seek, you may have to kiss that goodbye with some of these anorexic units. To save money on electricity most of the homes are lit by natural light which, of course, means lots of open exposed spaces. Welcome to the new millennium.

Jobs & Education. A cursory glance in the newspapers shows that hiring is mainly taking place in the tech sectors, leaving very little chances for someone with training elsewhere to secure a permanent position in a large company. Can the government afford a school loan forgiveness program? Perhaps it'll be expensive in the beginning, but in the long run, the community would reap the benefits. Personally, it doesn't bother me at all if Mr. Fancy Executive takes home $1,000,000/month; however, it's a pathetic egotistical show if all that money is simply spent on jet planes, golf clubs, 3 star Michelin restaurants and 5 star hotels around the world. One can only hope that some of his money is being donated to the needy in America and around the world.

As the internet grows, so will the reaches of Wi-Fi technology. Wi-Fi is pretty much available around the world but there are still some impoverished places where it is as scarce as running water. One current grant-making concern that is the leader in supporting initiatives for education, world health and population is the Bill & Melinda Gates Foundation. In addition to agricultural development, they also provide opportunities for medical and other professionals to ply their trade on an international stage. They are but one of many organizations where people can volunteer or get paying jobs while helping out in the betterment of mankind. Idealist.org, http://www.idealist.org/ claims to be the world's best place to find volunteer opportunities, nonprofit jobs, internships and organizations working to change the world since 1995. Give them a gander if you're interested.

R.E.S.P.E.C.T. One sunny, cloudless afternoon with only a minor chill in the air to remind me that winter only just exited a few weeks before, I sat outside the QFC on the hard, unforgiving sidewalk with two of my street friends. They were spánging, complete with a cardboard sign the size of a double LP which stated "Please Show Mercy to the Poor" or something like that. I wasn't begging like they were, simply sitting lotus style on the bird poop splattered concrete soaking up the sun. And you know what? If looks could kill it'd be a ghost writing this chapter now. A few people walking in and out of the store glanced at us with such hatred that all you could do is feel sorry for them; they don't know it but they could be keeping us company on the sidewalk tomorrow. Quite a few folks never bothered to look at us or even acknowledge that we were crouched there. And yes, there was the usual, "Go get a job!" jab. We never tire of hearing those because, like I always say, anyone walking past us could just as easily be down on their luck.

You know, I hate to admit it, but some of my street brothers and sisters could stand to straighten up a little to earn some respect. I suppose I can't fault people for ignoring the homeless who smell like a fast food dumpster exploded on them; I suppose I'd ignore them too if my senses were assaulted like that. So, with that observation out of the way, here's something else I think would benefit us:

24hr Drop-in Centers and Shelters with kitchens, lounges and showers. Is that asking too much? At least now, if someone smelled like a French sewer, they can't complain that there are no services available for them to clean up. I'm guessing that the atrocious state that most shelters are in is purposefully like that to discourage people from being homeless; if not, shame on the government for housing people in such deplorable conditions. It's no wonder some people prefer sleeping on street grates or beneath clothes dryer exhausts, basking in the warmth of their conditioner-scented steam. Of course, no drop-in center would be complete without social services, including access to psychiatrists, psychologists and medical professionals. They'd also benefit from job and educational opportunities, too. Some of these centers maintain a needle exchange program; some are even going so far as to have separate places where active addicts can shoot up without fear of being arrested. This is a new development, one they've been experimenting with in Portugal for years. Whether such a ground-breaking idea takes root here bears watching.

CHAPTER 32
Us *vs.* Them: The Good Guys *vs.* the Bad Guys

"I was homeless for about eight months. I refused to live with my dad or anyone for that matter. So I stayed somewhere that had no hot water, ever, no heat. I told myself I have to be strong and get through it on my own." Eric West, actor.

Believe it or not, some homeless people actually do care about the environment. Yes, I know. Every time you see a picture in the newspaper about a homeless camp there's garbage everywhere including broken wine bottles, burned out pots & pans, ripped clothing, dirty plastic bags, wrinkled tarps, bright orange needle covers, skid-marked drawers, graffiti'd walls, cans of empty spray paint, cans of empty Four Loko, chicken bones, vacant blister packs, full metal buckets of urine and so on. I'd be remiss to blame widespread littering on the homeless because it appears that people from all walks of life don't give a toss about Mother Earth.

For myself, I believe in leaving as small a footprint as possible. When I wash my face, brush my teeth and cut my hair in public bathrooms I always clean up after myself. I really go out of my way to make it look like I was never in the restroom at all. Why? Because the manager could easily follow behind me and, not only ban me from using the room, but ban all the homeless from using it. That's how it seems to work out here on the street. The whole group gets blamed for the actions of a few. Occasionally, occasionally, I clean up after homeless folks in public places. I don't do that all the time because it's tiring and, if we do get banned from using a particular place because of the negligent actions of a few, I can't say we don't deserve it. It sucks, but that's how it goes.

From time to time, and it does warm the heart to see this, some homeless folks will berate their brethren for leaving a mess and not cleaning up after themselves. Usually, a man who's made his home in the same park for 20 years or so would lecture someone new who discards his empty can of Coors on the lawn. That old geezer is proud to have lived in the park all that time, and by golly, no one's gonna come along and spoil his living arrangement for him. And you know, it's a shame: it's predictable that, if you set aside one section of a city park for the homeless to stay in, they will turn it into a landfill in no time flat. That's in stone. Sometimes you will see another homeless brother come along and shake his head in disappointment at the filth, but those kinds of people are few and far between.

I read recently that the city of Anchorage is considering paying the homeless to clean up their camps. Technically, that's ridiculous. You have to pay adults to clean up their own mess? Apparently, it would kill some people to push a broom or wash some clothes. Alaska WorkSource is behind this proposal. Their plan would be to hire the homeless at minimum wage and drive them around to clean up the various encampments in the city including, of course, their own. That's actually a good idea because no matter how many times you tell people to straighten out their personal rubbish, It. Ain't. Gonna. Happen. Right now, in Seattle, there are about 150 encampments on the city's "to clean" list. Theirs is a coordinated effort involving the Dept. of Parks & Recreation, Seattle Sanitation Services, WSDOT, Potta Porty Rentals, and social service agencies like Union Gospel Mission or Downtown Emergency Services Center (DESC), made complicated by the fact there are often human feces and used syringes to be picked up, folks to encourage to accept social services, and storage of items that someone may want later, like medicine, wheelchairs, photographs, etc.

On the City of Chicago's Official Site, there's an answer to this question: Why do people litter? Here's what they say.

1. People litter because they do not feel responsible for public areas like streets and parks. The more they litter, the more it becomes a habit, and the worse the community looks.

2. People usually litter outside their own neighborhood where their trash becomes someone else's problem.

3. People litter because they believe someone else -- a maintenance worker or responsible neighbor -- will pick up after them.

4. Once litter starts to pile up, people feel even less responsible

for adding to the litter. If an area is clean, people are less likely to litter.

The Boulder, Colorado organization Keep America Beautiful (KAB) has a more psychological reasoning in their answer to the littering question. To wit:

According to the KAB, Littering in America: National Findings and Recommendations by Wesley Schultz and Steven Stein (2009), there are various reasons why people are inclined to litter, from contextual variables to personal variables. Contextual variables can include the availability of trashcans, the accumulative impact of other litter in the area, and even weather. Personal variables include age, awareness, attitudes and feelings of personal responsibility. Stein and Schultz's study showed that 15% of littering behavior had to do with the contextual demands and 85% had to do with personal variables, the most commonly littered items being cigarette butts, food waste and wrappers.

Me? I was leaning towards good old fashioned laziness, but I suppose that's too easy. I wonder how many people would call me a lunatic for walking miles with an empty gum wrapper or empty can of pop until I could dispose of them properly in a garbage bin. Actor Matthew McConaughey once said, "There aren't many things that are universally cool, and it's cool not to litter. I'd never do it." Amen to that, brother. I'm reminded of the old Native American saying: "We do not inherit the Earth from our ancestors; we borrow it from our children." In other words, we'd better take care of Mother Nature if we truly love our children otherwise they'll suffer from the consequences of our pollution and destruction. The Earth is not ours to abuse. As Yoda might say, "Save the Earth, we must." I wholeheartedly agree.

***

I like scavenging and scavenging likes me. I think in one of my past lives I was a hyena or a vulture – the clean-up guys, the janitors of the Serengeti; had to wait to eat till the last lion sucked the marrow out of the gazelle's bones and drop what's left on the plains. It must suck being a hyena, though, because you're so ugly none of the big cats chase you. Your hind legs are short and your front legs are long. It's like you're pretending to be Eddie Murphy in Trading Places.

Someone in your family tree was definitely asleep when they were handing out beauty molds; he woke, finally got to the end of the line, and they gave him whatever was left – a mold from the suit that once belonged to Oscar Pistorius. You remember him, right? Blade Runner? Can't go jogging through New York City because of the grates in the sidewalks? Blew up the fireworks trailer on the Lord of the Rings set because he asked the wizard how to go home? Laughs at his friends when they hit the slopes because they have to buy skis? Yeah, that one. Hopefully, in his next life, he'll do better at the Olympics because in the last one he only had his sights set on the silver.

Anyway, back on topic. You do the environment a great favor when you scavenge. I used to rummage through the rich neighborhoods; in essence, I still do, but I really don't go out of my way like I did in the past. In Chapter 12, I spoke about some of the items I've found so there's no need to go over those again. But, to me, there's a psychological benefit to unearthing new stuff. Besides given you something to do to pass the time, you do get to see a lot of new sights if you're into that kind of stuff. I walk around these posh neighborhoods and I realize that, you know what; I may not be in a position or have the years to go back to school and earn the necessary degrees to get a job that could buy one of these homes, but it doesn't matter. I wouldn't live in such a big house by myself anyway. I live hand to mouth, and that's okay, because I'm able to appreciate that the little I do have is better than the nothing some people own.

CHAPTER 33
Protect Yourself *from* the Evil That Men Do

"My family was actually homeless for several years when I was a kid. It's a bit unusual for a member of Congress." Kyrsten Sinema, U.S. representative from Arizona's 9th congressional district.

Hey, gents and germs, guess what? Not all my homeless brothers and sisters are saints. Horror of horrors! Yep, some of 'em can be downright mean and dirty, the kind you definitely don't want your daughter dating or the creepy ones who take pleasure in staking out your neighborhood in the middle of the night. So, what is a self-respecting, rent paying, hardworking, tax paying, voting registered, dog walking, public display of affection having, amusement park visiting, car owning, bicycle riding, tree hugging, iced caramel macchiato drinking citizen such as yourself supposed to do if the homeless grim reaper comes knocking on your door? Well, for one, you don't open your door. That's a no-no. First, you ask, "Can I help you?" If he says something arbitrary like, say, "My car broke down and I need to use your phone to call AAA," politely tell him, "Sorry. I can't do that." You could always claim you don't have a phone but he won't believe it even if you really don't. Simply lying to him turns his anger up a notch. Unfortunately, Superboy at your front door isn't going to leave that easily. Plan on him being persistent while you continue to stand your ground.

"Ma'am," he'll insist, "I knocked on every door and no one's home except you. I really need your help. I'm a barista at the Starbuck's on 23rd St. I'm sure you've seen me there before. I probably waited on you." He'll then produce an ID to drive home his point. So far, he'll sound legit, but don't fall for his subterfuge; he's an expert in the art of bullshit.

"Sorry," you repeat again, "I can't help you. There's a corner store just up the road. They'll help you." You've just told him all you're prepared to say; now, whatever happens next will tip your little conference to the left or right.

First, the right scenario: He says, "Sorry. Didn't mean to disturb you," then turns and leaves. As you peep through the slit in the curtain and watch him disappear from sight, you breathe a heavy sigh and put the Louisville slugger back up against the living room wall.

Second, the wrong scenario: He says, "Lady, I really, really need your phone. I'm not leaving till I can get some help." That's when you immediately dial 911. Arguing with this chump will get you nowhere. You've said all you've had to say; now, your congress has taken a left turn. Call 911 and tell them there's an intruder at your door. If Superboy overhears your phone call, he'll cuss you out but he'll bounce. If he didn't, tell him you'll call the police if he doesn't leave. My suggestion is to call 911 anyway since it's hit or miss whether the police will come or not. (Yes, I've had the experience where I once called 911 for a belligerent homeless drunk who was threatening people in the street and calling me all kinds of nigger, and I waited for 2 hours and 15 minutes, and the police never came. I also had a friend who was grabbed on her breast and threatened to have her head bashed in, so she called 911. After an hour of waiting I simply drove her to the police station to file her report).

Do I advocate gun ownership? Soitenly! I think every home should have one, unless the homeowner or renter is perpetually depressed and unstable like me, then he'll just use the gun on himself. Some burglars won't take no for an answer. Depending on their desperation, they'll either try kicking your door in or breaking a window to gain entrance to your fortress of solitude. Unless you can fight like Sammo Hung, forget about going one on one with this joker. Some of these people have such a long history of drug abuse that sometimes tasers and stun guns don't stop them from assaulting you. As a Jain, I don't advocate violence; however, as a Jain, you are allowed the right to defend yourself and your loved ones. In other words, should he forcefully cross your threshold, bring out your friends Smith & Wesson. They'll never let you down.

You don't have to be in your home to be harassed by my more hopped up brothers and sisters. You could be out walking your tiny Affenpinscher in Volunteer Park one calm and soothing morning when, suddenly, from out of the bushes, Homer the Hobo runs towards you with what looks like an apple corer in his right hand. Since your little pooch's bark is much worse than her bite, she can't help you keep this joker away. If you'd previously learned self-defense, then by all means, drop this fool to the ground then run for help. If you're a master of the spinning crescent kick, perfect. Use it or lose it. But if you think a roundhouse is a place where Eskimos live, keep that pepper spray handy and don't be afraid to spray like a kid with a lisp. Homer's fiending for a hit, and by golly, you're going to help him get it. Or not. Now that his eyes are on fire, maybe he'll change his life around for the better. Give yourself a pat on the back for giving this ruthless runagate a push in the right direction. Some folks, unfortunately, understand nothing but tough love, so don't feel bad if he starts rolling around on the ground from the pain and call you names you'd need to look up their meanings for on Wikipedia someday. You're helping him get his act together and that's a good thing. Your generosity will remove negative karma off your soul while keeping Dennis the Menace off the street. Not bad for a day's work.

Giving money to people just because they ask for it is a simple form of extortion. I know; that's a pretty brutal thing to say, right? Extortion is actually the practice of obtaining something, especially money, through force or threats. But you know what? Some people are scared of the homeless and figure it's better to give them money than say no, just in case they get pissed and call them names or even attack. I'm homeless and there are homeless people I avoid because they really are bad eggs. I would say, though, in general, don't tell a vagrant to get a job if they're panhandling. You really don't know who you could set off in the wrong way and he suddenly gets Chuck Norris on your ass. Some transients are very fragile and unpredictable; in the blink of an eye, they can go from Mother Teresa to Lizzie Borden. So, if you give money, try to view that as a truly genuine activity as opposed to fearing the beggar. They're just trying to survive, just like you. Remember, you can go to work one day, your boss intercoms you, "Paul, can you come to my office?" You walk in expecting to hear how great a worker you are, but instead, he slides an envelope over to you on his desk. "What's this?" you ask. "Your last paycheck," comes the reply. Not exactly what you wanted to hear. Don't worry, though. We'll keep a good spánging spot in front of the 7-11 warmed up for you. You're welcome.

Every day, just walking down the street, any street, I see a potential distress call to Safelite Auto Glass. If you've left your laptop or smartphone on a seat, you can kiss them goodbye. If there's a box or bag in there, someone might break in and hope they get lucky. I knew a guy who left a box of bibles in the back of his car. When he went out to the parking lot the next morning, all the glass from a rear window was scattered on the ground and the box was just a few feet away from the car, and yes, all of its contents still in place. Obviously, the burglars were interested in money, not religion. Someday someone's going to install flame jets beneath their Mercedes Benz. As soon as a tweaker presses his fingertips on a window peeking into the car, the jets will ignite and fricassee him so fast there'd be nothing left to identify except his dentures. Heaven help him if he was toothless from chewing Skoal for over thirty years or so. Steering wheel locks and burglar alarms are also good deterrents; at least they're more street legal than those flaming fire jets. New lesson to learn: look out for people walking around with leather marble bags filled with ball bearings. They can break through car windows relatively quietly with that setup and suck out your GPS or CD/MP3 player before you come back from buying that pack of Marlboro Lights at the gas station.

Here's another tip: never, ever chase someone who snatched your purse. Just let the police know. It's their job to apprehend these thieves. Last thing you need is a bullet in your shoulder or a letter opener in your spleen. Despite common perception, spleens are a good thing to have. You need it for producing and removing blood cells, storing platelets and white blood cells, and helping to fight off certain bacteria that cause meningitis and pneumonia. Beware, though, of those newfangled $100 handbags whose handles wrap around your wrist. Bad idea. I saw them in a women's magazine when I went to see a doctor the other day. They look chic and fashionable and may well complement your Luly Yang outfit as you're strolling through crime-free Dubai; stateside, however, is another matter. It'd suck to have your wrist dislocated just because some rapscallion is trying to boost your expensive Christian Louboutin lipstick, Yves Saint Laurent touché éclat highlighting pen or whatever people keep in their clutches these days.

CHAPTER 34
So You Think You Got Problems?

"I notice how well or badly a guy treats a waiter, or whether he's kind to some people and not to others. One guy I was with actually yelled, "Get out of my face!" at a homeless man. Needless to say, there was no second date." Sarah Wynter, actress.

I'm grateful for every day I get to wake up and see what's going on. Seriously. How many of us are guaranteed tomorrow? It'd be better, though, if every waking day I didn't find myself at war with myself. Every morning, if you listen very careful through the soothing whistling of the whippoorwills and starlings flitting through the pines, you can hear the faint sound of a roaring crowd screaming, "Let the games begin!" That earnest crowd of spectators you hear very clearly is coming from my head, their teeth gnashing with the expectation that Robin would have a spectacular war with himself. It never fails. They noisily place their bets as they watch the two contestants in my head, my emotional-minded amygdala who I call Lizard Boy because he is the lizard brain, and logic-implementing prefrontal cortex, Pre, take their corner of the ring and get ready to fight.

I'm telling you, the constant fighting can get downright dirty sometimes. And I never know who will win – Lizard Boy or Pre. Both try their level best to control my actions because both are necessary for my survival, yet both are responsible for the torments I face every day. Lizard Boy is all action and has the patience of a crackhead – he wants what he wants, not now, but right now. Pre is a little more laid back. He likes to take his time in ascertaining all conditions that are placed before him. It's almost a futile war, really, because in the end Lizard Boy is usually the victor.

There's a substance Lizard Boy loves very much – dopamine. He can't seem to get enough of it. He loves it when that neurotransmitter floods the brain during a satisfying meal or sex act. And of course, if ultra-dopamine is introduced to the brain via external means such as liquor and drugs, Lizard Boy is as pleased as punch. He's so content that he prefers the monster dopamine hit over the childish food/sex hit and try his best to keep the powerful dope coming. Bad, bad boy. His erratic behavior often creates anxiety, depression, schizophrenia or bipolar disorders in unsuspecting folks who were otherwise fully functioning, normal people. Enter the psychiatrist with his satchel of pills. Does he have what ails the troubled mind? Hopefully, but psychiatry is not an exact science because not much is still known about the brain.

The clerk at a local gas station, for instance, told me it took 20 years for the psychiatrists to get his depression medication right. 20 years? That seems like a relatively long time to me. A lot can happen in 20 years. To wait for a more manageable mood that length of time seems utterly cruel.

And so, here we are, out on the street, strolling past disoriented people who, we guess, sometimes incorrectly, don't know up from down, left from right, wrong from right, black from white, night from day. Their world is a diminished vortex of confusion and uncertainty, infamy and blight. Where to eat? Where to sleep? What to eat? Very disturbing. And yet, it is these very people which are often the fodder for the comedian's trough for ages.

Who doesn't love a jester, a clown or a fool? You see him pop up everywhere, doing things that normal people eschew. All have names, but only a few become famous – Rigoletto, Till Eulenspiegel, Dagonet, Clopin Trouillefou, etc. Some of these buffoonish characters are simple minded and some are dark and mysterious. No doubt, the models for these literary characters were probably real people with serious mental health issues, with some sent to their unjustly deserved deaths for being "witches", "devil worshippers" or "cursed."

They say we all have a twin somewhere, a doppelgänger just itching to be found. Over the years, I've ran across quite a few people who seem to have a twin in another city. They may not be the same race, age or gender, but boy, do they have the same mannerisms down to a science. Here are the descriptions of a few I've met.

The Eccentric Lady. This woman, who ranges in age from about 30 to 70 or 80, has an annoying habit of stopping traffic by running into the street, flaying her arms like she's signaling semaphore flags, and then suddenly bending down to pick up smoldering, discarded cigarettes or some other items before moving along. She is, of course, in her own little world and would prefer if no one intruded into it. You couldn't if you tried anyway because talking to her is like talking to a wall. She might answer a question directly, but often, her answers make no sense, as if she's just throwing words out and hoping something sensible sticks. She eats anything, regardless of whether she found it on a bus stop bench, in a garbage can, by the curb, in a parking lot, or gazebo in a public park. Most people who glance at her occasionally don't wince until they see her peeling off the used bubble gum stuck to the glass or column in the bus shelter and chewing it. I think every city has an Eccentric Lady or two.

Trouble, Walking. Nobody likes Trouble, Walking. He's a pot-smoking, meth-loving paranoid young man in his 30's or 40's with stubble on his chin and a humongous chip on his shoulder. His clothes, often military-styled, doesn't fit correctly, and his tattoos, all clumsily applied by himself with cheap India ink, are negative in nature. Trouble Walking's behavior includes pooping and peeing on public bathroom walls, drawing graffiti everywhere, stuffing the public toilets with yards of paper till the room floods from over-flushing, yanking the toilet paper dispenser off the wall and leaving it in the flood, constantly arguing with people about inconsequential nonsense, jumping up to, then dangling, off stores' signs in the streets, and breaking the windows of parked cars.

He's been to jail a few times and has a serious hard-on for the police. He is suicidal but will probably challenge the police to put him out of his misery some day because he hasn't the melons to do it himself. If he was a child, he would probably be labeled as having ODD – Oppositional Defiance Disorder. As an adult, my guess would be BPD, but that's just a guess. It could very well be he's garden variety batshit crazy. Who knows?

The Rainbow Lady. Have you ever wondered why some people, notably women, wear layer upon layer upon layer of super colorful, mismatched articles of clothing as if their personal dresser was Helen Keller? Their faces are usually decorated paint-by-number style – a little blue here, a touch of red here, a streak of gold here, a dash of green there. You can't tell where their rainbow-hued hats, shirts, bodices, dresses, skirts, robes and scarfs begin and end. It's as if they were strolling beneath the scaffolding of twenty artists painting "The Last Supper" high up on the side of the Continental Hotel when all the open cans of paint suddenly fell off the scaffolding and onto them. I'm sure these ladies think they look like Elizabeth Taylor in "Cleopatra", and maybe in their eyes, they do. I'd never walk up to any of these women and tell them their combination of colors shoots a sharp, dental-like pain into the back of my skull; after all, life is short. These ladies are pretty harmless and self-expression is a personal thing anyway.

The Cigarette Smoking Man. Obviously, I'm not referring to the recurring character from "X Files". This other guy walks around all day collecting half-smoked or ¾ smoked cigarettes out of gutters, garbage cans, parking lots, public parks, ashtrays and potted plants in order to indulge in what's left of the fine tobacco in them. Nothing screams "desperate" more than someone's willingness to mesh a stranger's smoke-tainted spittle with theirs, unless you count the guys who go around town drinking what's left in the beer bottles and cans left near the dumpsters. You can't fault anyone for doing what they do; after all, what kid raises his hand in 2nd grade and says he's gonna be a used-cigarette recycler when he grows up? Things just happen and it does no good to look down on the desperate. Anyone can be in their shoes.

The Shopping Cart Lady. The quintessential model of homelessness, Ms. Shopping Cart Lady is the one always featured on the cover of national magazines like "Homelessness Now", "Dumpster Chronicles" and the Pulitzer Prize winning "Bread Line Digest". You can spot her from a mile away; she would be the one who looks like she packed up a cabin and somehow forced it into one cart. How Shopping Cart Lady is able to maneuver such a monstrosity is beyond comprehension. It is amazing she can find anything in her oversized carriage at all. If I was to sit and rattle off everything she carried, I'd be here till NASA's Juno hits Jupiter.

She is a kind, albeit solitary, soul, who always seems to be in need of cough medicine and a solid place to raise both her legs to allow the water that's been collecting in them for years to finally drain out. Sometimes you can see her talking to herself or the one-eyed cat that lives in her cart, sometimes she turns on her 1950's transistor radio to listen to big band music, sometimes you see her sleeping standing up, propped up against a supermarket wall. She is a classic and will always be around to grace the cover of your favorite hobo magazines.

Speed Sister. You know the one: can't sit still, talks at 60mph, very jittery, always in motion, speaks too loudly, makes unusual gyrations with her hands, wears un-matching clothes, asks for assistance for something then suddenly veers off into a different direction, has long unkempt hair, dried up pockmarks on her face, arms and legs, always intent on bumming a cig from anyone and everyone, and is just a heartbeat away from kissing all the rest of her rotten teeth goodbye. Speed Sister used to be such a good girl. Had high marks in school, was a popular cheerleader, went to church on Sundays, visited her sickly grandparents every month, always remembered to brush her teeth and walk the dog whenever her father asked her to. How did she turn from Daddy's Little Girl into the poster child for Zombies Anonymous?

Well, it's a sad, and common, story. Daddy was a little *too* friendly with her, if you know what I mean. Her uncles weren't much help, either. The young man she hoped to marry someday turned out to be a loser who introduced her to whatever drug was popular in school at the time, then suddenly dumped her at a stranger's meth lab when she became too much to handle. And of course, Speed Sister did whatever she could to survive on the streets – peddle drugs, turned tricks and robbed johns. After several hospitalizations and jail bids, she ended back out on the street. She no longer uses; instead, she's now permanently burnt. Cigarettes and the occasional sip of wine seems to keep her comforted along with the meds her psychiatrist prescribed. Speed Sister has a future, just not out on the street. With a little more attention from social services she may be able to get turned around.

The Falling Down Drunk. You've got to feel sorry for these guys. They're perpetually grimy and dirty with leather for skin due to being exposed to the elements, especially sunlight, time after time. Some have never seen a shower in years, so yes, they will smell like they were foraging in the storage bin at Waste Management. Contrary to popular opinion, these guys do eat...once in a while, but what really keeps them going is their liquid diet of liquor, liquor and liquor. There are many reasons why they ended up where they are – divorce, loss of a job, can't get a job, evictions, bad tempered, etc. Most people are able to transcend these setbacks and get on with a normal life; others are plagued by mental issues like PTSD, intellectual disability, schizophrenia, borderline personality disorder, Autism and depression which, unfortunately, keeps them out on the street perpetually.

You'll notice I didn't say 'laziness'. That's the #1 insult people scream from their cars as they drive past these lost souls. *"Stop being lazy! Get a fucking job!"* And that's especially if one of their co-workers is blind with one leg and the other has the arms of a sparrow. Do you think any street person would stop, scratch their head confusedly and wonder, "Wow, get a job? How come I didn't think about that?" The Falling Down Drunk doesn't care too much for the world anyway. Their quest for booze keeps them occupied enough.

From the moment they wake up from wherever they passed out hours before, the hunt is on. If there is no beer or whiskey in their immediate environs, they'll resort to begging, pride be damned. Yes, most people do shun them, walk around them like they are a cesspool of filth and, if looks could kill, there'd be smoldering piles of ashes where they spánged. But, you know, I could understand that people don't have the time to play Nobel laureate to these down and out guys, and I'm not saying that citizens should support their extreme alcoholism, but there is the reality that anyone can lose hope and end up on the street especially if they have no network of support.

Mr. Know-It-All. Do you know which character you'll most likely encounter in a homeless camp – the ultra-smart, has-all-the-answers-to-the world's-problems-but can't-secure-his-own-apartment-because-every-landlord-in-town-is-prejudiced-against-him kind. He can tell you the secret history of the town you're in, who the streets were named after, which countries in the world has the best leaders and those with the worst, which mountain in India is the easiest to climb and what is the best tasting beer in Belgium (and he knows this, of course, because nobody knows what to look for in a craft Belgian beer except him). He'll also reveal to you, oh unsuspecting reader, who the best actress in Hollywood is, the breed of dog most appropriate to raise in the suburbs, and last but not least, who the best host of The Tonight Show was. Pretty smart guy. Why is he wasting away in an anonymous homeless camp instead of making big bucks as a staff writer for Jeopardy? Oh, that's right. He hates that show. He also hates sunny weather. He hates the fact that "they" will steal his ideas and not give him any credit. And ever since he was a kid he's always hated L.A. because he could feel it in his guts.

Mountain Man in the City. (If you're just like me, "Hot Child in the City" by Nick Gilder should be playing in your head right now). You know this guy; well, not personally, no one does, but you see him everywhere, forever dressed like the lead in the Rip Van Winkle musical. He has a white navel-length beard, floppy, dirty hat, crumpled dirty clothes, muddy old boots and looks just like a walking bag of bones.

No one knows where this 60 or 70 or 80-year-old man came from, how he got there, what his plans are, where he eats, sleeps or relieves himself. He talks to no one and seems to prefer it that way. But you're always surprised that when you do ask him a question, he answers it with lucidity and promptness. And you're always tempted to ask him questions: Why did you resign yourself to living such a solitary life? Do you have kids? Where is your family? Where are you from? Are you the Unabomber? What's your name? Even though he's mysterious, he seems harmless.

He doesn't drink or smoke in public and you'd half expect that, if you see him go around a corner, and you quickly ran after him, he wouldn't be there at all, like a ghost disappearing in the night. He is a sad figure because, when he dies, he ends up in an unmarked grave with the other Joes; very common sight.

The Seasons MixerUppers. These guys perplex me to no end. During the winter, with snow and ice on the ground, and the air so crisp you can write your name in your breath, you see them walking around casually in t-shirts, some even just wearing shorts. I don't know how they do it, but they do and the freezing temperature doesn't seem to faze them at all. And, like the mysterious Mountain Men, they share the same trait - appear and disappear into thin air like a will-o'-the- wisp. During the hot summer, you see their cousins who are dressed like this: fur-lined parka with the hood up, snow goggles, some wearing gloves, padded waterproof trousers and thick leather boots.

The great, albeit mysterious, pianist Glenn Gould was one of these guys. In the middle of the summer he wore scarves, coats and gloves. He was even arrested because the cops thought he was a vagrant. Some of the conditions Brother Glenn could have had might be anemia, hypothyroidism, hypochondriasis, OCD, all contributing to his frigophobia – the persistent, abnormal and unwarranted fear of coldness. Or it simply could've been he thought he was the bomb when he dressed like Jeremiah Johnson, who knows?

The Rooted Man. Here's an interesting, Jabba the Hut-like character you'll find almost everywhere. Weighing in at nearly 500 pounds, The Rooted Man just doesn't have the strength to move from his secure position beneath a bridge or roadway. Why should he move anyway? Everything he owns in the world is on the ground around him and on the blanket upon which he sleeps. This guy is so large and immobile that people are surprised he's even alive. As a matter of fact, passers-by who do see him often wonder if he's dead. Tragically, he could be. Feel free to walk over and drop a quarter or two into the cowboy hat he has positioned right in front of him. The tinkling sound may stir him…or not. The hat should be right next to the rusty old thermos, half-empty bottle of orange juice and VHS copy of 'Jurassic Park' next to his shopping cart. You may not be around when he wakes up, but in his heart, he appreciates the money.

The Bird Man. That would, of course, be the animal rights guy who frequently stops in his tracks just to whip out a few slices of bread, granola bars or crackers to feed the local urban fowl like he's an employee in a public aviary. All of his friends, whether they be pigeons, ducks, crows, geese or gulls, recognize him when he comes walking up the road, often pushing each other aside to be the first to feast. (There is no magnanimity in the animal kingdom, at least not with birds). Bird Man appears to have a special affinity with the ornithological critters, as if he can read their minds. In some cities, the little feathered flyers often perch themselves on his head or shoulders, such is their blinding trust of him. Tourists who love that visual presentation enough to take pictures sometimes give him money. Bird Man seems harmless and can probably be approached without caution. Probably.

The Self Talkers. Disclaimer: I'm not making fun of these guys. People who walk around talking to themselves are most likely stricken with schizophrenia, a brain disorder in which people interpret reality abnormally. According to statistics from the Department of Health and Human Services, 600,000 people are homeless. Of that number, 200,000 have schizophrenia; one third – seems kind of high. Well, then, let's see. Even though I spend a lot of my time alone, I do have a few homeless friends I socialize with sometimes. It's weird to think now that, out of the nine homeless people I know, three of us are schizophrenic. (I say 'us' because the jury's still out on that diagnosis in regards to me). None of us in the group walk around talking to ourselves, but in the homeless population I am associated with, there are two women and two men who carry on continuously as if they're guests of Dr. Phil. My guess is they're from 25 to 55 years old. They're all casually dressed and all keep to themselves. Very often, though, when they are asked simple questions, their answers are so left field that people simply give up and move on to someone else.

In all my years of being homeless, I'd say that most of the perpetual self-conversationalists I've encountered are harmless. Yes, some do scream out suddenly and with such profanity they have to be escorted out of buildings by security guards, and some do talk so loudly to themselves that those standing around often yell back but, generally, the general population just ignore them, at least here in Seattle anyway where self-talkers are a common sight.

One day, purely as a social experiment and learning exercise, I cruised around downtown Seattle talking non-sensibly to myself loudly and on purpose. I adopted a few self-talker traits such as laughing suddenly, moving my arms awkwardly and without intention, altering my gait from time to time, staying in motion while waiting for the walk signal to come on, keeping my eyes to the ground and occasionally making off the cuff comments at things I saw, like kiosks, fire engines, hotels and so on.

Hopefully, from all my years of being homeless and being a patient in different psych hospitals, my performance was convincing. Charlie Chaplin used to emulate the gait and motions of strangers on the street and incorporate those movements into his films. That was the intention of my experiment: to see how strangers responded to my actions. In the end, no one viewed me with disdain or contempt. No one shouted at me, tried to rob me, push me down, mock me or taunt me. As a matter of fact, after my hours-long experiment, I was disappointed that I was practically ignored. Maybe they were scared of me, I don't know. But that was a good thing. I see now that the self-conversationalists are accorded the same rights in society as anyone else who is not misbehaving, and at that, I can't complain. Hell, I'll admit I need some schooling myself especially in regards to new issues such as 'Queer.'

Victor/Victoria. For years now I've been familiar with the term LGBT – lesbian, gay, bisexual and transgender. Sometimes I see LGBTQ and thought the 'Q' part meant questioning. It does, but it also means 'queer.' I'd thought gay and queer were the same thing. Apparently not. From what I've been reading, queer means you don't "identify" as male or female, irrespective of what "parts" you have. Even with possessing the components of a female or a male, queers don't consider themselves either. In fact, they eschew pronouns such as 'he' and 'she' and just go with 'they.' Sexuality, I understand, is on a spectrum, and so is gender.

The definition of "identifying" as queer is a concept I'm still wrapping my head around, especially in reference to androgyny which means actually having the sexual characteristics of both male and female. For instance, if I called myself Angus McTavish, ate haggis, wore a kilt with ghillie brogues, carried a bagpipe all day, and identified as being Scottish, that still doesn't make me Scottish. I am, ¼ Chinese and ¾ black regardless of how I "identify". In any case, I don't feel like I fit in that much with either group, something I explain further in Chapter 37.

Being on the street these days I've been learning a lot about the queer group because, unfortunately, many of them, especially queer teens, have such a hard time in life that they do end up homeless. Some of the other terms I've been getting a grip on lately include 'non-binary', 'gender fluid', 'pansexual', 'metrosexual', 'androsexual', 'cisgender', 'demisexual', 'gender non-conforming', 'bigender', 'pangender', 'genderqueer', 'skoliosexual' and many others. I won't be surprised if the acronym 'LGBTQ' disappears. Lately, I've been seeing QUILTBAG – Queer (or Questioning), Undecided, Intersex, Lesbian, Trans, Bisexual, Asexual (or Allied), and Gay (or Genderqueer). I don't know who came up with QUILTBAG but I like it a veritable quilt of different colors and simpler to say than LGBTQ. Works for me. Now, how about if we get these people off the street, huh? Sidewalks are for getting from hither to yon, not sleeping.

CHAPTER 35
Famous Homeless People

"If my fans want to do something for me when that time comes, I say, don't waste your money on me. Help the homeless. Help the needy...people who don't have no food...Instead of some big funeral where they come from here and there and all over. Save it." B.B. King, blues singer and guitarist.

And now we come to the part of the book I subtitle "Keep Your Head Up, You're In Good Company," or for those you into Earth, Wind & Fire, *"Keep Your Head to the Sky."* If you're into Argent, it's *"Hold Your Head Up."* But, once again, I digress. Sometimes life is easier to bear when you realize there are others in the same boat as you. Some of the people mentioned below became homeless and died that way after a life of creativity, and some achieved greatness after being down on their luck for a while. Life goes both ways; there is no algorithm for success. BTW, in this section, when I talk about being homeless, I don't mean those who couch surfed or stayed in their friend's garage; at least they had company and some support. I'm referring to those who slept alone in buses, cars, parks, under bridges, in the streets, airports, in doorways, and other places not suitable for human habitation.

Steve Harvey – He was homeless for three years, living in his car, eating expired food pantry vittles like his fellow street contingent. I'm sure back then people probably used to look him up and down as they walked past with criticizing eyes. Now he's a multi-millionaire comedian and talk show host. Not bad, really, considering his humble past. I'm sure he doesn't take his riches for granted because he knows in the blink of an eye he could be right back to square one, keeping Robin company around the fire in an oil drum on Rockaway Beach.

Tyler Perry – Another guy who lived in his car before he made it big as a movie writer, actor and director. When you sleep in your car you have two choices – lie scrunched up in the back seat or reclined in the passenger seat. Scrunched up in the back is good if it's freezing outside or you don't want people to know you're actually back there getting a few Z's. Your knees will hate you for it, though. They can only stand that position for so long till they start reminding you, painfully, not to do it again. Sleeping reclined in the passenger seat is good if it's really hot outside or you're just trying to nap. Naturally, you don't want to leave any open containers lying around just in case a state trooper comes rolling by.

Kurt Cobain – You know, I feel bad for this guy. He really was good looking with beautiful golden hair and a nice smile. He also wasn't too shabby a guitarist, singer and songwriter, either. But those demons he harbored would dog him for the rest of his short and miserable existence. Kurt was known for his anger tantrums as well as his drug abuse. It probably didn't help that he slept under bridges; that could only fuel a man's desperation to escape the morbidity of his reality even more. Dying at 27, he would join that elite group of famous musicians whose lights went out at that tender age – Jimi Hendrix, Janis Joplin, Jim Morrison, Robert Johnson, Brian Jones, Amy Winehouse, and many others.

Sly Stone – Is he still alive? A recent tabloid hoax gained traction when it claimed he'd passed. He's still kicking, though, because Brother Sly has more lives than a clowder of cats. He lives out of his van in L.A., presumably enjoying the $5M he won from a lawsuit last year. Now let's do some math. One eight ball of coke costs around $80 in L.A. If you're a superstar like him it'd just cost $70 and an autograph. $5M will buy you 71, 428 eight balls. If his habit was as bad as Whitney Houston's, or worst, Rick James', he'd be averaging 4 to 5 eightballs a day which, at that rate, would last 14,285 days or 39 years. But that's for the average Joe; superstars are not like the rest of us. Sister Whitney spent $7M on drugs over a period of 12 – 15 years. That means, in one year, she would've done enough dope to give a fleet of elephants a right sided hemiplegic stroke. Too bad. Mental disability is a bitch; it really bites. Hopefully, when I finally do cross over into schizophrenia, I won't be aware of it. If I start stripping naked and climbing the flag pole outside the governor's mansion with a rose between my teeth, I hope I won't know. Should you ever see me skinny dipping in the cesspool at the back of Safeco Field, do me a favor and put me out of my misery, please.

Edgar Allan Poe – the great mystery and horror writer died homeless. I used to be a big fan of Poe back in the day. Once upon a time I had even memorized his poem "The Raven" because I liked it so much. I also remember those afternoons spent watching Vincent Price in movie adaptations of his works such as "The Pit and the Pendulum", "The Raven", "House of Usher" and "The Masque of the Red Death". Poe was one of a handful of people that inspired me to be a writer; Ayn Rand, Ivan Turgenev, Franz Kafka, Judy Bloom, Upton Sinclair and John Steinbeck were a few of the others.

Nikola Tesla – physicist, electrical engineer, mechanical engineer, inventor, all around cool guy. How bad could you have been if David Bowie chose to portray you in a movie, right? Tesla may have been on the autism spectrum too because of his noted visual and special acuity, among other things. The jury's still out on whether or not he died broke and homeless. Some say he died in a Manhattan hotel, some say he was homeless. I don't want to erroneously perpetrate the myth of his homelessness, but if he was, that wasn't such bad company to be in.

Moondog – He was in interesting fella. Called "the Viking of 6th Avenue", Moondog was a poet, composer, musician and inventor of several musical instruments such as the trimba, a triangular percussion instrument. His real name was Louis Thomas Hardin and was often found on 6th Avenue in NYC between 52nd and 55th Street busking in his Viking-style outfit. Before you dismiss him as just an eccentric oddity, notable composers like Philip Glass trace their influences back to him, so if he's good enough for Philip Glass, he's good enough for me.

Religious leaders – Jesus, Buddha, Mahavir. I guess it's a requirement that if you're going to lead people out of darkness, it's best to have a "do as I do" and not a "do as I say" approach. As a Jain,

I'm a follower of Mahavir. He was a handsome Indian prince with a wife and child when, at 30 years old, his parents died and he decided to leave home and live an ascetic life by himself. For the first 12 ½ years he meditated, stayed naked, fasted and underwent severe austerities. After that he became an enlightened one, a Jina, and also became a teacher and founded an order of monks and nuns. I couldn't live an ascetic life in the U.S. because the minute I strip naked and start walking down Main Street I'll get arrested. As inspiration then, Jains look up to their monks and nuns because they have adopted a life of severe austerity and penury. I think that makes it easier for me to accept the fact that homelessness is not as bad as it seems; in fact, it's a virtue when viewed from a different perspective, or *anekantavada,* as the concept is called in Jainism.

Jewel – Being homeless is bad enough, but for women it's downright dangerous. There are some days I say to myself, "You know what, self? You're lucky to be a man and not a petite woman like, say, Halle Berry or Jennifer Lopez (both of whom were also homeless, by the way). Jewel lived in a car for an entire year after she was fired from her job by a boss who wanted sex from her but she refused. Since she didn't get her last cheque, she had to scrape by just like the rest of us on the street and obtain her sustenance from food banks, missions and churches.

Like a trooper, she didn't give in to the vicissitudes of street life and kept on practicing and performing where ever and whenever she could. Hopefully, one day, she'll write a book about that one year she lived on the street and talk about all the stuff, good and bad, she went through. I saw her perform briefly, I believe, either at Lupo's Heartbreak Hotel or the Roxy in Providence. I didn't pay to go in; the door was open so I just stood outside and watched. It was just her with an acoustic guitar. I didn't know who she was at the time; it wasn't until the next day I read in a local paper how she was on a solo tour promoting her first album by giving free shows around the country. Beautiful woman. Glad I had the chance to see her live.

CHAPTER 36
Movies About Homelessness

"If you ever go to Temple Square in Salt Lake City, if you stay there long enough, you'll see a homeless person standing in the middle of their nice, beautiful square, holding out a cup for change. And the Mormons don't ever ask him to leave." Trey Parker, actor, animator, screenwriter, director, producer, singer and songwriter.

One particularly blistery winter, I drove from snow-on-the-ground Providence to sun-drenched L.A., the land of enchantment and wonder. The southern, and extremely picturesque, route I traveled on took me five days. I probably would have arrived faster if I'd had a car that was in better shape than my 15-year-old Pontiac T1000 which I'd called Sandy after the woman I'd purchased it from. Sandy was relatively reliable but she sure needed a lot of care. Her main, and loudest, problem was her misshapen rocker arms. You could hear me coming from streets away. Those solid metal arms rattled so loudly against the engine's head that they used to awaken animals hibernating by the interstate. Since I only had $300 on me, I couldn't afford to fix it, so I just spent money on Lucas Heavy Duty Oil Stabilizers all the way down I-40 (or Rte. 66 as they called it back in the days when you could shake hands with the devil and promise him your soul in exchange for seven years of wine, women, song and fame).

Obviously, because the engine was so bad, I couldn't drive as fast as I'd like. It came as a surprise to me, then, that I was pulled over just 10 miles east of the California Border. I'd just left Flagstaff, zooming down this steep hill in complete free-fall. The patrolman said I was doing 84 in a 75. Me? In this car? Sweet! He said he's not going to give me a ticket because I was so close to California and, chances are, I wasn't going to return to Arizona to pay it. Nice chap. He did ask me if I was smoking weed. I told him no. He said he couldn't believe that because I had a Bob Marley sticker on Sandy. I told him, "Me luv reggae, mon, but me nah bizness in ah ganja, seen?" He let me off with a warning and I just continued on my merry way.

I'd driven to L.A. to write movies, get rich, buy an estate next to Steven Spielberg and go shopping down Rodeo Drive with Janet Jackson and Meryl Streep. Well, I never met Meryl nor Janet, never bought the estate next to Steven, and never even got rich. I did manage to write a few scripts, though. I'd immersed myself in the art by spending a lot of time in the AMPAS library on S. La Cienega Blvd. AMPAS is the Academy of Motion Picture Arts & Sciences, but we Hollywood insiders just call it AMP. (No, we don't. I just made that up).

I'd written five movies in the 2 ½ years I lived, albeit homelessly, in L.A. They were *"Strung Out"*, *"Iron Maiden"*, *"Tears of a Clown"*, *"Stranded in Paradise"* and *"Diamondback."* The 6th, *"Little Hammer"*, was just in treatment form. I never did make a full script out of it but I was able to turn it into a short story which was eventually published a few years later. I did make a few contacts in La-La Land but they all basically panned out. The closest any one of my scripts came to production was "Tears of a Clown", a horror film. The old-school producers disliked my "Iron Maiden" script because it wasn't in traditional three-act, linear/arc form. I cited "Pulp Fiction" as its influence because the continuity of that movie makes no sense, yet it was a blockbuster. They didn't want to take a chance, though. Oh well. All is not lost. I can always produce it later if I find out where John Gotti left his stash of unmarked bills he'd hidden just before going to prison.

In scriptwriting school, they say to write what you know. Right; tell that to George Lucas who, I guess, must've spent a lot of time on Alderaan because he seems so familiar with it. Nevertheless, if there's truth in that axiom, then I probably should've spent all my time writing about homelessness since I'd experienced so much of it over the years. As it turns out, I really don't have to because many movies with this familiar theme had already been produced, from small Indies to big studio projects to foreign language ditties. These kinds of, usually sympathetic, films are easy to find, too. Just look for flicks with titles that include words such as "vagabond", "tramp", "drifter" and "wanderer" and you'll be right on track. I omitted comedies like *Trading Places*, *Down & Out in Beverly Hills* & *Pretty Woman* because they're trite and unrealistic. I want to focus on the more serious offerings, so without much further ado, I now take a look at a couple of films about homelessness. Watch 'em and weep.

Midnight Cowboy. That's a good 'un. Jon Voigt and Dustin Hoffman were spot on. Jon Voigt plays Studley Doo Right (or whatever his name was) from Oklahoma or Texas (I forget which) who figured he'd come to NY to sell himself to single, rich, bored, undersexed ladies who are just starving for some good loving from a blond, blue hunk such as himself. Of course, it doesn't take that long for dreams to go from beautiful fantasy to realistic mess as he soon found out when his money and his hopes faded into evanescence like cigar smoke. Out of necessity, he turns tricks with guys in midtown Manhattan while trying to stay in the good graces of his pickup friend, sickly Dustin. ("I'm walking here! I'm walking here!") This film lays out in plain, disturbing images what hopelessness looks like – the dark basements, eerie johns, smelly bathrooms, crumbling spires, rat infested abandoned buildings, everything that'd make any sane-thinking stud from Oklahoma or Texas think twice about visiting the Big Apple without already having a good setup.

My rating: 4 cans of tuna, 1 can of spicy black beans, 1 loaf of sourdough bread and a package of cupcakes only two days old.

My Own Private Idaho. It's been a while since I've seen this Keanu Reeves/River Phoenix/Gus Van Zant film, and like most of the movies I've ever seen in my life, I was most likely under the influence of something. If anything, I remember the B-52's song "Private Idaho" better than this flick. Anyway, this is really my $.02 about these films. Obviously, much better reviews can be gleamed from Rotten Tomatoes or IMDb. Just don't go by the ratings on IMDb. Studios pay people to post excellent reviews about suck-ass films on IMDb, so you just have to go through them with a fine-tooth comb. The quality of the film will eventually reveal itself. MOPA is about a friendship between two homeless street hustlers in Portland, Oregon. River is the younger one and he's besieged with narcolepsy. Keanu's the older guy who teaches him the ways of tricking. This movie is worth watching because River was cute but his flame burned out too quickly, like Anton Yelchin, the 27-year-old Russian actor

("Star Trek", "Odd Thomas") who died this morning when his car rolled and pinned him against a mailbox in his driveway. Keanu, like Tom Cruise, Johnny Depp and Brad Pitt, is just getting a free ride through Hollywood because he's handsome, but if he's your cup of tea, by all means, watch MOPA. The only thing that bothered me about the film was how River and Keanu were portrayed as angels; not really angels, but definitely not the drug-addicted, pock-faced, crime-addled, potty-mouthed, non-trustworthy hustlers I've ever met.

My rating: 2 cans of tuna, 1 loaf of bread and a box of Sun-Maid raisins.

The Soloist. This was a good 'un, featuring Jamie Foxx as a homeless schizophrenic street violinist/cellist and Iron Man (Robert Downey, Jr.), a yuppie journalist who befriends him. By the way, before I continue, just one question: Is it redundant for a homeless person to watch movies about homeless persons? That question reminds me of when I used to drive a taxi in NY. I was instructed to pick up a fare at Newark Int'l Airport in NJ from upstate NY. It was a long trip but I would be recompensed accordingly. I arrived at the airport and took my place amongst the well- dressed limo drivers who were also waiting for their fares to arrive. I felt ghettoish standing amongst these perfectly groomed chauffeurs, sort of like I was tainting their holy space. Anyway, since I'm relatively invisible, no one paid attention to me. And what do limo drivers talk about, you ask? Routes. Yep, that's it. Routes – the fastest way to get from the FDR to the Holland Tunnel; the smoothest, less congested traffic from the LIE to the Brooklyn Bridge, and so on. Routes. Drivers...talking about...routes. Can you say BORING!!? But, I digress.

The Soloist was worth the price of admission. I thought maybe it was a little bit manipulative, but not cheesy, like syrupy 1940's dramas about soldiers returning from the war with an arm or leg missing. In any case, there was a lot I could relate to in the movie – the poverty, the musicianship, the city (I was homeless in L.A.), the loneliness and, of course, the mental illness. Like a lot of films, this one started off nicely then started limping towards the end. I realize Hollywood likes a return on their investment so they give movies a nice happy ending. Maybe I shouldn't be so cynical and accept that not every schizophrenic who ends up on the street will retire in Potter's Field someday. Maybe I'm just projecting.

Anyway, my rating: 3 cans of tuna, 1 box of corn flakes, and a one-day old sliced cucumber, tomato and feta cheese wrap from the Trader Joe's on 24th St.

The Grapes of Wrath. This was the movie that made me fall in love with John Steinbeck and Henry Fonda. You know, it's a shame that people have to put up with these incredible hardships just to get a buttered roll and a glass of milk. Tom Joad (Henry Fonda) and his family had to uproot from the dry as hell dustbowl that was Oklahoma during the depression and head to California where, hopefully, they can get jobs in the grape industry. Basically, TGOW was a road film where Murphy's Law was in full effect. People starve, people die, people wear despair like wet towels around their sunburned necks. And, to add insult to injury, when they finally do get to Cali they realize they were just chasing a pipe dream. There are no jobs. The dusty old flyer they'd found that brought them out there was just that, old, as in, get thee to another state; nothing to see here. Very depressing, pretty much homelessness in a nutshell. According to Wikipedia, when Steinbeck was preparing his novel, he wrote, "I want to put a tag of shame on the greedy bastards who are responsible for this [the Great Depression and its effects]." Remember that question I'd asked before? "Is it redundant for a homeless person to see a movie about homeless persons?" I'd say the answer is no because it always helps to see what other people in your shoes are going through, and it doesn't hurt to meet or see people you can relate to.

My rating: 4 cans of tuna, 1 can of peppered-corn, 1 can of low sodium green beans, 1 gallon of 2% milk and a bag of chopped romaine lettuce with French dressing.

Ali Zaoua: Prince of the Streets. That's right. America doesn't have the market cornered on homelessness. As a matter of fact, considering how prosperous the U.S. is, it probably comes as a surprise to people around the world that not everyone lives like the warm, sunny, white-toothed characters in Disney movies. For myself,

I was shocked, shocked I say, to see how some denizens of Kansas, specifically Norton, lived. I went to college in Iowa and made a friend who lived in Alma, Nebraska. During school holidays, I stayed with him and his family.

One weekend night we drove across the border into Kansas to meet his friends, or cousins – I don't remember which, in Norton. I'm a sucker for discovering new places, so I'll gladly go anywhere blind if it doesn't mean I'll take a .44 Remington slug to my face. Anyway, the people and house I encountered there completely threw me off guard. Call me naïve, but from what I saw in "Herbie, the Love Bug", "Snowball Express", "Mary Poppins" and any other Disney flick with Dick Van Dyke or Johnny Whitaker, Americans, especially white Americans, lived like kings complete with butlers and maids, streets paved with gold, sky blue swimming pools, faithful dogs, cars that talk, and homes so large you can park an 18-wheeler in the living room.

But here I was, in Norton, standing in the threshold of a hovel so dilapidated a strong fart could knock it do the ground. There was dog poop in almost every square inch of the carpeted floor; carpet, by the way, that looked like every drunken frat boy in a fifty-mile radius puked on it over a period of one year. You could easily see the Orion constellation through the jagged gaping hole in the unfinished ceiling. Torn sheets were strung haphazardly across the broken windows. Some of the holes in the walls had wads of newspaper stuffed in them, presumably to keep the raccoons living in the dark spaces at bay.

The inhabitants of the house, if you want to call it that, actually matched the décor of their humble abode - they were just as ragged, greasy, grimy, ornery, stoned and dirty. Disney World this was not, but to see it in America…that took me by surprise. In a foreign language film like Ali Zaoua, that kind of desperation is the norm. Set in Morocco, the film chronicles a brief period in the lives of street kids who, like other urchins around the world, learn to grow up fast just to deal with the harsh reality of their bleak surroundings. In their young age, they will be exposed to fights, sex, rape, drug abuse, prostitution, arrests, murder and utter hopelessness. Ali hits you hard because the actors are street kids, not Hollywood transplants. You can't fake that kind of desperation on Hollywood and Vine. Pixote, the Brazilian version of Ali, pretty much follows along the same lines. Pixote, shot in bold, vibrant, gritty Technicolor, is a young boy who is being used by authorities as a drug runner and mugger. Of course, we always know how these affairs end up. The endings are never pretty, and the stories are not wrapped up neatly with a bow and sold to the Regal multiplexes attached to sprawling malls. The homelessness of adults is tough, with children it's worse; in some countries, it's a killer. Just see the powerful, Sub-Saharan film War Witch and you'll understand what I mean.

My rating: 3 bowls of vegetables tangine, 1 couscous t'faya, 1 bowl of traditional Harira soup and a salad Marrakesh.

Ironweed. This is a relatively depressing, but sublimely interesting, vehicle for two of my all-time favorite actors, Meryl Streep and Jack Nicholson. The time period - Halloween, 1938. The city - Albany, NY. The mood - cold, harsh, unforgiving. The screenplay and novel were written by William Kennedy but it could as easily had been a John Steinbeck production. One thing I liked about this feature was that, even though the setting was 1938, it didn't look dated at all. In fact, if the film had been released this year, I would've believed it was shot on location in any modern desperate-looking town that just lost the one huge business that was keeping their economy afloat. It's a simple story. Jack is a drunk and Meryl's his paramour. Both of them just want to survive the brutality of their surroundings; it takes great effort, for instance, just getting warm or a few hours of sleep. It also doesn't help that the townsfolk resent they exist so, armed with baseball bats and torches, they attack the homeless camps in the middle of the night, burn their tents to the ground, and beat some of the campers into bloody pulps. Life for the homeless is no joke; this film illustrates that truth quite well; required watching for those sympathetic to the plight of their less fortunate kinsmen.

My rating: 4 cans of tuna, 1 bag of jelly beans, 2 Kaiser rolls, and 1 block of government cheese.

Will Smith. There is no movie called Will Smith. I only

mentioned him because it seems like he has a great interest in portraying the homeless on screen. He did it three times – *The Pursuit of Happyness, 6 Degrees of Separation* and *Hancock.* I haven't seen Pursuit yet but I did see 6 Degrees and Hancock. It's been a long time since I saw 6 Degrees, his first film, but in it he's a gay homeless shyster who pretends he's the son of Sidney Poitier so he can live at people's homes for free. In Hancock, he's a severely drunk homeless superhero who rarely remembers the catastrophe he creates until he sees it in news coverage later. One day, if I run into Brother Will, I'll ask him what's his fascination with playing homeless characters. I could only hope that the other powers that be in Hollywood take notice and bring more homeless characters to the screen. The more the merrier, I say. Both films are worth watching, BTW.

My rating: 4 cans of tuna, 2 boxes of Kraft mac & cheese, 1 package of freeze dried potato flakes and a fried egg sandwich from Tony's Italian Deli on Somerset Blvd.

The Terminal. Tom Hanks is one of those "can't miss" actors. It seems like all his roles are so important to him that he really becomes the characters he portrays, and that makes his films more believable. Cast Away is another "homeless" role he played that's worth mentioning although it's mainly about a man who got stranded on a small island with a volleyball he eventually started calling Wilson. In The Terminal, he's a man without a country. The east European land he wants to fly to is unstable, and because they're in the midst of a war, their economy is upended which makes his passport null and void. In other words, he's stuck at JFK till Slovakia, or where ever he's from, get their act together. I suppose there are worst places you can be homeless in, but JFK is a pretty big airport with lots of food and bathrooms, so it's not that bad. Plus, he befriends some of the airport personnel so he's not as super lonely as he was in Cast Away. I like films like these because they show just how much a person can take without going full-on bonkers, how resilient the human spirit can be when faced with ultimate challenges. Same as war films. With bullets zipping past your ears every few seconds, you probably wish, at some point, that one of those bullets would find a home in your skull. In Dante's Inferno, there are nine circles of Hell. In Jainism, seven grounds of Hell. If war is the deepest level of Hell, then homelessness is somewhere near the middle. At least, in Jain Hell, your soul can rise to one of the Heavenly grounds. It might take billions of years but it can be done.

Anyway, my rating for The Terminal and Cast Away: 4 cans of tuna, 1 package of dried curd cottage cheese, 2 cans of peaches, and 1 rectangular tin of crackers from Moldova.

Being Flynn. This is an indie drama starring Robert De Niro and Paul Dano. Before I continue with this review, I want to talk about Paul Dano's role in Prisoners. In that film, a father played by Hugh Jackman kicks the living stuffing out of the man, Paul Dano, who made Hugh's daughter disappear. Paul was right on point in that film; probably should've even been nominated for an Academy award. My biggest gripe about the movie, however, is we never see the major ass whopping Hugh delivered to Paul, just the aftermath. Paul looked so bad that you just knew he wasn't simply slapped around. I guess the filmmakers decided to spare the audience the visual torture of Hugh's brutally violent attack because they wanted us to sympathize with Hugh losing his daughter and not see him as an unrelatable monster. Anyway, back to Being Flynn. Paul Dano is an aspiring writer who works at a homeless shelter where his alcoholic father, Robert De Niro, stays. Their relationship, of course, is strained. There's more tension between the two of them than a ball field full of pitbulls. Okay, that's a bit exaggerated since they're not trying to yank each other's tracheas out. Still, no "Leave it to Beaver" this is. It's a cute and realistic little film with a happy ending. Julianne Moore's also in it if that'll help you rent it. Required viewing? Well, if you see it, that's cool. If you miss it, no big deal. There are worse ways to spend 90 minutes of your free time.

My rating: 3 cans of tuna, 1 sesame seed bagel, and 2 cups of Dannon Oikos Raspberry Greek yogurt.

Journey of Hope. War and extreme poverty creates homelessness. If I were to review, for instance, all the foreign language films that dealt with those two issues alone, I'd be here forever. City of Life and Death, for instance, is one excellent example

---

of this. It's about Japan's Rape of Nanking, China in 1937. 300,000 Chinese soldiers and citizens were killed mercilessly and many had to flee for their lives. When you think about it, most road movies are technically about homelessness because, in your quest to go from Point A to Point B, you will end up sleeping in your car, or motels, or the woods, parks and rest stops like I did. At least, in my five-day drive from Rhode Island to California, I didn't have Japanese war planes dropping bombs on me like they did to the escaping Chinese refugees who, incidentally, survived by resorting to cannibalism of those who'd already died and also making feline stew and canine meatballs out of their pets.

Journey of Hope is a joint Swiss-Turkish production. A poor Turkish family decides to leave their impoverished village and set off to Switzerland, a country that gladly opens its door to the desperate when necessary. Naturally, nothing goes as planned. If their trip wasn't long and arduous enough, the impenetrable blizzard in the Alps simply existed to remind them theirs was not a fortunate circumstance. Add to that, sleeping in caves and dealing with shady human traffickers, and you can imagine what I mean. I'm not going to say too much about what else goes on since there is joy in discovery and I'd hate to ruin anyone's experience of viewing it. The movie did win the Academy Award for Best Foreign Language film back in 1990 so that alone should tell you how great it is. Even to this day it still stands head and shoulders over the thousands of films I've seen in my lifetime, and I'm proud to place it on the same shelf as these other attractions – Amadeus, Disney's Beauty & the Beast, Finding Nemo, Jean de Florette and Manon of the Spring. If you haven't seen it yet, staple it to your bucket list. You won't be disappointed.

My rating: 4 eggplant moussaka plates, 2 Abdullah kebabs, 1 bowl of kunafe with ricotta cheese, 1 Swiss Reuben, 1 demi-poulet rôti à la broche, 1 frozen carpaccio de bœuf aux copeaux de parmesan and a free coupon for 1 Salade Campagnarde avec jambon cru du Valais, gruyère, œuf dur et noix from Chalet Suisse on South Boat St.

Shogun Assassin. I obtained this DVD title from a public library; I don't remember, though, if I'd borrowed it from Providence, Hollywood or Nashville. I'd never heard of the movie or the manga it was created from ("Lone Wolf and Cub"), but since I'm a sucker for martial arts films, I thought I'd give it a looksee. (It also helped that the package said "Strong" and "Uncut"). The titular character, Ogami Itto, was the shogun's executioner (a master decapitator, really) but his wife was killed by the Yagyu clan, so he and his young son, Daigoro, become homeless assassins on a quest to revenge her murder. This movie was a surprise find because I had no idea "Lone Wolf and Cub" was already so popular in Japan. According to Wikipedia, the manga was first published in 1970, then it was adapted into six films (Shogun Assassin is basically a portmanteau of the first two movies), four plays, a television series, a new version in 1992 called Lone Wolf and Cub: Final Conflict, an American version which was announced in 2012 by director Justin Lin and a video game. Wikipedia also says it's widely recognized as an important and influential work. You can see references to it in Quentin Tarantino's Kill Bill and Frank Miller's Sin City and Ronin series.

In addition to the storyline, swordplay and fountains of blood, the electronic instrumental music near the end of Shogun also captured my ear. It sounded like something Tangerine Dream would do. Unable to find the soundtrack anywhere, I simply recorded that part of the movie's audio and walked around playing it over and over. When they said the movie was "Strong" and "Uncut", they weren't joking. Ogami was no angel, that's for sure. Maybe an angel of retribution, the kind you'd never want to meet out on a desolate street in the middle of the night, but not an angel with beautiful white wings and a soft cotton robe. I think the Japanese director Takashi Miike could have been influenced by "Lone Wolf", too. Some of the extreme graphic scenes he creates for his horror movies and war epics are reminiscent of it, a tribute if you will. Yes, you do need a strong stomach to handle Shogun Assassin, but if you can get past the decapitations and dismemberments, you're in for a journey.

My rating: 4 spicy tuna rolls, 1 mini tempura udon, 5 pieces of gyoza, a package of Agedashi tofu, and 1 packet of Organic Sencha Japanese green tea powder.

Time Out Of Mind. This is a micro-budget film that stars Richard Gere in a role you rarely see him in, someone poor and out, in New York City, no less. He's a homeless alcoholic who does appear to have the knowledge of how he came to be on the street, but not why. He's estranged from his family, including his daughter, who he tries to reconcile with intermittently during the course of this 2hr drama. Time Out Of Mind took me five or six days to watch because it plods along like a rhino pregnant with twins. I had to view it in 15-20 minute intervals; any more than that and I'd be snoring here in the Northgate Mall or Library. Everything in this movie I've basically seen, if not, experienced. In fact, if a film was made of a week or two of my life in homelessness it'll pretty much look like this. I do understand the reason for the movie's lethargic pace, though. The filmmaker wanted the audience to feel Richard's character's ennui as he tries to circumnavigate the morass that is the NY social services and shelter system. At least he made a friend, albeit short-lived. Such is the disappointment of living on the street. Because this presentation showed homeless life exactly as it is, without Hollywoodisms, I do recommend it

My rating: 3 cans of tuna, 1 can of baked beans, 1 can of pork & beans, 1 box of crackers and a tall can of Cheese Whiz.

Addendum: I was going to include a chapter in "You Can't Sleep Here: A Clown's Guide to Surviving Homelessness" called Books About Homelessness, but the truth is, I haven't read any. I've had my paws on many social service pamphlets, Real Change newspapers, drug addiction memoirs, survivalist brochures, soup kitchen maps and magazine blurbs, but never a book specifically about foraging and sustaining yourself in the streets. There are a few, though, I'd like to read in the future such as "Rachel and Her Children", "Tell Them Who I Am", and "Street Life Under a Roof." So, once I get my sticky fingers on those, hopefully from one of those 'Little Free Library' cabinets since I'm perpetually broke, I'll include their reviews in my next homeless book – if I'm given the chance to write one.

CHAPTER 37
Health Care *and* the Mentally Ill

"I'd been in Sacramento a day and already noticed the pervasiveness of its homeless problem. The city seemed like California without the masks or pretense; a place where dreams were occasionally made but mostly torn apart." Tom Bissell, journalist/critic/fiction writer.

I am an aberration, an abnormality, a freak of nature, what they would call el bicho raro in the hills of Cordoba or kawarimono in downtown Tokyo. People like me were never intended to live for a long time or have a normal life. Either we ended up in circus side shows or became street clowns who did tricks for money or were burned at the stake for being possessed by demons. I "belong" to quite a few disparate groups but I am still an outsider to each of them.

I'm black, yet I feel a disconnect with other black folks because I'm an atheist where a majority of black folks are Christians. I listen to metal as opposed to most black folks who enjoy hip hop, R&B, and contemporary jazz. I have no interest in "typical" soul food which constitutes meat dishes such as ham hocks, fried chicken, ox tails, ribs, steak, crawfish, catfish, etc. In fact, I eat no meat at all, whether it's fried, baked, sautéed or fricasseed. Black-eyed peas taste "blah" to me. Cornbread makes me choke to death. I have no interest in grits. Collard greens are bitter though not as bad as mustard greens. I skip root vegetables such as yam, potatoes, carrots, turnips, cassava, onions and ginger because it's again Jain beliefs. Since I have very little interest in sports, activities such as boxing, soccer, basketball, baseball or whatever holds no interest to me. Also, just being gay automatically makes me an outcast to the black community. There's also the sad reality that, when I was growing up, most of the people that made fun of me, pushed me around, attacked and mugged me, were brothers. Consequently, and this sucks, I'm forced to keep my distance from urban neighborhoods out of fear. Believe me, I feel guilty saying that, but that's how it is. And then there's colorism, the idea that lighter skinned blacks have it better than darker skinned blacks. There have been many movies and articles on this subject, and unfortunately, I've been a victim of it which, of course, forces me away from my own community. Here are links to some articles about colorism:

https://en.wikipedia.org/wiki/Discrimination_based_on_skin_col or

http://www.bustle.com/articles/37427-5-truths-about-colorism-that-ive-learned-as-a-black-woman-in-nyc

http://www.tolerance.org/magazine/number-51-fall-2015/feature/what-s-colorism

http://colorismhealing.org/colorism-films-movies/
http://colorismhealing.org/

I'm also Asian-American – I'm part Chinese – but there's a disconnect with them, too. This is difficult to summarize without sounding racist so I'll try my best to be as politically correct as possible. Most Asians, they say, are notoriously clannish. I don't know whether this is true or not but I have heard and read that a few times. I look more black than Asian and, therefore, usually get lumped in with those who are outsiders to the Asian community. Also, since I don't speak Chinese, I can't very well communicate with those who do in the International District and elsewhere. I'm attracted to Asian guys; this fascination with them probably started when I used to watch all those Shaolin movies with Wang Yu, the hottie from Hong Kong.

Over the years, I've sought to date Asian men. As there weren't very many around me in the places I've lived, I've had to rely on online dating sites and ads from weekly newspapers. Their ads were always disappointing, to wit: "Asian bottom seeks hot white top" or "Asian guy seeks his Mr. Perfect. Whites only, please", etc. The ads I placed looking for Asian guys, sadly, were never answered, and this was years of looking all over the place. To be fair, I did have two 'sort of' Vietnamese boyfriends, and the Asian drug addicts and dealers I associated with in Seattle were Vietnamese, so I really can't complain, not when it comes to the Vietnamese, anyway.

I'm gay but there's a disconnect with the LGBTQ+ community, too. I've gone to several gay bars over the years in NYC, Provincetown, Nashville, L.A. and Seattle...and got ignored in most of them, probably because I'm not a hunky stud, a cute twink or a burly bear. I did meet a Hungarian guy at Hatfield's in Queens one night but he was so drunk he would've went home with a can of crawfish and not know the difference. I've always felt like an outsider to the gay community, whether I was hanging out on Christopher Street in NYC or Capitol Hill in Seattle. Consequently, I've attended no gay pride parade ever. As it turns out, I can't do crowds anyway because, to an autistic person, all those lights and sounds are like battering rams to their skulls. I handled meeting people better when I was drinking since alcohol dulled my senses, but now that I'm sober, it's just difficult for me, that means no parades, no conventions, no rights marches. My reception in gay community centers had been no better, either. I once went to an AA meeting at a gay center in Capitol Hill. Everyone simply walked around me like I was imperceptible; not a soul said hi. I give up. And then, this is a sad fact, there is racism in the gay community. I'm not making that up. I've linked to some sites where you can read all about it.

 http://www.huffingtonpost.com/news/gay-racism/
 http://www.towleroad.com/2016/03/michael-sam-2/
 http://www.pinknews.co.uk/2015/06/11/80-percent-of-black-gay-men-have-experienced-racism-in-the-gay-community/
 http://people.ucalgary.ca/~ptrembla/gay-white-racism/2-white-racism-america.htm

I'm autistic which, by definition, makes me a social misfit. Some folks with Asperger's are able to assimilate into the masses, maybe even get married, have spouses and kids, but I wasn't so lucky. I have the social skills of Mjölnir; I couldn't keep a relationship going unless I paid them off. My brothers and sister are of the same stock as me but the Asperger's shtick places me in a whole different ball park, the "Wrong Planet." I can relate to Aspies well if it's online...somewhat; however, in person, I have the same social issues with them as I have with NT's (neurotypicals, the normal folk). And since Aspies tend to be non-wavering, very black & white and inflexible-thinking people, conflicts can easily arise there as well. Fear of a black planet? Try fear of an Aspie planet. We'd probably kill each other by the time we get around to electing our first leader.

I'm from Trinidad & Tobago but there's a disconnect with my fellow islanders. Trinis are a religious, Christian, hetero lot. Bad for me. When I was growing up you were either black or east Indian. I was mixed and, therefore, the target of bullies.

This kid once told me on Monday, in school, that he was going to beat me up. Why? I don't have a clue, so I ignored him. On Tuesday, he repeated his threat. I was confused about why he was picking on me; again, I ignored him. Wednesday came, Thursday came and I believed he'd left me alone. On Friday morning, he saw me and repeated his threat. As before, I just ignored him. That afternoon, after school, as I was walking home, I heard a commotion coming from a couple of yards behind me. Glancing back, it was the kid who'd been threatening me all week surrounded by curious onlookers. I continued on my way home but did start getting a little anxious after it seemed the crowd behind me was picking up its pace. Then, when I made a right onto my street from the main road, the kid suddenly jumped on top of me from the back and started punching away. I tried shaking him off but it didn't work. Somehow, I was able to reach into the book bag I kept on my back, withdraw a refill pen, and push it into his neck. Screaming, he jumped off me and ran across the street. As I was getting myself together to run home, he picked up a half empty bottle of Guinness stout and threw it at me. He missed. Instead, it struck the wall by the hospital I was standing near and its foul-smelling content splashed on my clothes. Of course, I started running like crazy and was relieved to know he didn't bother following me up the hill.

Looking back, I've often wondered what that kid had against me. I did nothing to him. In fact, I was so quiet I barely spoke to anyone in school. Even back then I isolated. And, since I wore glasses, that alone kept me out of playing sports. (If I had accidentally broken my glasses my father would've removed my ribs with his bare hands). I've always wondered if it was my light-skinnedness that played a part in me being picked on. I also felt the same kind of negativity when I came to New York and when I went to Nashville to write country songs years later, the whole colorism issue I'd spoken about earlier in this chapter reared its ugly head.

I like to sleep in the safest neighborhoods I can find. Here in Seattle, by luck or design, they just so happen to be white areas like Magnolia, Maple Leaf, Wallingford, Royal Heights, Queen Anne and so on. I try not to stay in the same place because I do think a lot about the residents there. No one will come tap on my window and say, "Um, sir, I hate to disturb you, but your sleeping here outside my house makes me nervous. Can you please move?" Yet, I feel like I'm trespassing. How can I not? For that brief moment, I'm the fly in the ointment; I kinda stick out like a sore thumb. Since residents know I can sleep on any unrestricted street for three days, I can legally sleep in front of their houses. I'm sure they don't like that. "Honey, do you see that guy sleeping in his car out front? The nerve! We paid half a million for this property and he thinks he can just waltz in here and settle in like he owns the place? Gimme your shotgun!"

There was an issue recently that the mayor of Seattle addressed in the newspaper. He talked about how some apartment buildings don't rent to, or give a hard time to, gay and black folks who are looking for a room. There was an undercover investigation done which revealed this fact. Seattle's not the only place, either. I'd faced this same issue before in NYC, Kingston, NY, and Hollywood; I don't think I have to go around from town to town to find it exists everywhere. The internet abounds with these kinds of stories. Because I feel like I'm trespassing, I try to maintain a low profile in those quiet neighborhoods I rest my head. I'm not going to be on earth much longer. The least I can do is finally relax in an area that pleases me, mortgage be damned. All I've got to do is remain cool, stay calm, don't make any waves, and drive off when the morning sun comes up, or the birds awaken...whichever comes first.

You'd think that, me being homeless, I'd find comfort in hanging out with the homeless. I did, in the past, during my drug and alcohol heyday, but now that I'm clean I prefer to be by myself and away from the influences and temptations that can bring me back to square one. I don't hang out with the smokers because the fumes just make my eyes water (I wear contacts, and when the smoke gets trapped under them, it is hell on earth for me). A lot of homeless people smoke weed and drink alcohol; I don't. Forget about the heroin addicts, meth heads, crack heads, mushroom heads or what have you. They're a no-go. I stopped eating in the soup kitchens because they don't serve what's appropriate for my Jain diet. Practically all their dishes have meat, and that's a no-no. So, who's left? Well, I suppose I can always hang around the schizophrenics; then again, they're in their own little world and they tend not to let anyone in. Besides, being schizoid, they already have company to talk to 24 hours a day; three's a crowd. You know, now that I think about it, I wish they did have a pill for schizophrenia; not to take it away, to give it to those who want it. Swallow one of those puppies with a glass of water and you'll never be alone again. Think of it as an anti-loneliness pill, for those times when you just need a friend.

Last but not least, I'm a Jain, a follower and practitioner of Jainism, the oldest living religion in the world. Originating in India, there are currently between 4 million to 6 million Jains in the world, most of who live in India. The rest are scattered throughout the world, including the United States. Most sects worship in temples; some eschew both temples and idols altogether, taking our concept of aparigraha (non-possessiveness) to its logical conclusion.

Jainism is an extreme religion and requires certain sacrifices from its adherents. Since our main tenet is ahimsa (non-violence), we vow not to harm or kill any living thing, even including plants. One natural example of our practice of ahimsa is our diet. We will not eat any kind of meat. We reject root vegetables in our diet because to harvest them will kill the entire plant. In other words, no potatoes, carrots, onions, garlic, cassava, or yams. We eschew honey because it is regurgitated spit and food stored and intended for bees. We reject drugs and alcohol because minute animals are killed in their production and they taint the mind, causing it to stray from its path of non-violence.

There are four distinct followers of the Jain sangh or order – laymen and laywomen, monks and nuns. The ascetics are the monks and nuns. Us laypersons learn from their incredible sacrifice – they own nothing, not even clothes (Digambar monks, anyway). They beg for food. They've renounced their friends and families for the ascetic life. They spend most of the day in meditation and, from time to time, fast as penance. Since they don't travel, there are no monks or nuns in the U.S. To become an ascetic, you'd have to travel to India, mainly Gujarati, where Jains are concentrated. Therein lays my problem.

Over the past two years, since becoming a Jain, I've been reaching out to the local Jains to guide me and give me instruction in the scriptures. This has been a slow-going process because most of the Jains here in Seattle are Gujarati and speak little to no English. The ones who do speak English are married with jobs and kids and have no time to play school teacher with me. I do attend some of the main holidays at our temple in Bothell, but in all honesty, I still feel like an outsider to the community. Since I have no Jain friends, simply acquaintances, I am left to study the complex canon on my own. This, itself, has been a difficult practice because almost every Jain I contact on the internet claims, "Study this book. This is the main one," while someone will say, "Study this book. This is the main one," and so on. Since it seems like every book is the "main book" I've simply put my energies into studying, by myself, the original book that all Jains agree upon as the topmost and definitive, the Tattvartha Sutra. Boy, it sure is lonely at the top.

I said all of that to help explain the roots of my severe depression, anxiety, bipolar manifestations, and drug & alcohol abuse. As it turns out, among the homeless, my story is not so unusual at all. It's kinda really the norm. Many of us out here were abused as children. Many are autistic. Many are drug and alcohol abusers. Many suffer from depression, anxiety, schizophrenia, bi-polar disorders, you name it. Some are on medication, some are not. Some are so far gone they're just like asteroids floating around in the miasma of cosmic incertitude. These people will never make it home and will die as nameless as the spaces they inhabit. The positive in all of this is psychological and psychiatric help does exist. In fact, a brand spanking new building even opened up recently in Seattle where the old Community Psychiatric Center used to be. It's called Valley Cities – Meridian Center for Health and they're currently looking for customers. Maybe I'll give 'em a call.

CHAPTER 38

The Lost *and* Found

"I knew a homeless guy who gave all the copper coins that people gave him to charity. So I think there's something that makes us want to give. For me, it's quite a selfish luxury: you feel enlivened, deepened and self-nurtured by generosity." Tamsin Grieg, actress.

I have absolutely no idea why I created this chapter, after all, what do we have to lose besides our minds? Being homeless is as low as one can go in life. Apart from the clothes on your back and the frayed shoes on your feet, that's pretty much the bulk of your possession. Sure, some of us protect our paraphernalia like they were the family jewels, but I doubt that was the gist of this chapter. Perhaps I was thinking about altruism when I wrote 'The Lost & Found'. Some religions and cultures believe, as do I, that karma exists. If you do something good for others, something good will happen to you. If you do bad, keep a sharp lookout over your shoulder because you don't know when a piano will come crashing down on you from the sky.

Anyway, back to the topic at hand: the lost & found. When you're a stray you've lost more than just a home, more than just a place to scratch your post. Besides the possibility of losing friends and family, you can sometimes watch as your dignity gets washed down a drain like maple leaves in the middle of autumn. With despair comes hopelessness; with hopelessness comes drug and alcohol abuse. That can signal the beginning of the end for a lot of people. That light at the end of the tunnel seems farther and farther out of reach with each passing day. Long gone are the days when you woke up in the morning, smiled a dazzling smile, and thanked the gods for bestowing another day upon you. Now, when you wake up, you think, "What?! Another freaking day of torture?!" Pretty soon those active train tracks start appealing to you more and more.

Losing is not pretty; in fact, it's downright depressing. You walk around the streets of the city looking as lost as a shark in the desert. Everyone passes you by; you're just a blur to them, a non-entity, a figment of their vivid imagination. You're sure that if you doused yourself with gasoline and lit a match, no one would notice the conflagration. Then there are those times when you're sitting forlornly in the street and someone does notice you and, out of the goodness of their heart, offer you an apple without realizing that you don't want food because you don't want to be kept alive. All the apple does, then, is perpetuate your angst, your misery and your pain. "Thanks," you say, "but I don't want it. I'm starving myself to protest the horrible living conditions in Darfur."

If there's one thing being homeless teaches you is how to be strong. Every day brings with it a new uncertainty. Is this the day the police bust me for sleeping on the park bench? Is this the day I break my legs jumping out of a dumpster? Is this the day the food that the yuppies left out on the magazine kiosk is laced with arsenic? Is this the day I lose my life to Homeless Harry and his schizophrenic cousin, Mack the Knife? Maybe this is the day I finally get robbed of all my possessions, prompting me to finally take to that bridge like I'd planned. American Express used to claim, "Membership has its privileges." Naturally, they didn't mean membership in the Homeless Club; still, there are quite a few things you find when you're undomiciled.

There's an unbelievable freedom that comes from being on the street. For myself, I'm not confined to just a 400-sq. ft. apartment. My living room is this entire town. There are several places I can just chill in and write on my laptop. I have many bathrooms to choose from. Since I'm surrounded by people all the time I'm never alone. In fact, being alone was one of the worst things that befell me. Loneliness forced my hand into binge drinking and drug abuse; there was no one to check on me or admonish me for my transgressions. Now, I'm in public 24 hours a day. In a sense, I'm being supervised but my neighbors just don't know it.

And of course, there's the bit about me not having to punch a clock. It's taken me my whole life to realize it, but I wasn't meant to go to school. At all. It was a total waste of time. I didn't fit in in any academy I attended. Perpetual outcast, I. Everything I learned about reading and 'riting, or most everything, I taught myself. I wasn't supposed to apply whatever useless education I had to a job because I was never meant to have a job, either. What was I going to do? Live the American dream? Buy a house, have kids and a spouse, get a dog, buy a boat to sail around the Puget Sound with and count my stocks and bonds every night till my eyes bled? As it turned out, school and working were nice ideas, just not for me. I'm too weird for that, too left of center. They tried to shove this square peg into a round hole but failed. Nice try, though.

Some cities are better than others to be transient in. L.A. was torturous. I wouldn't even let a dog be homeless there. There are no shelters, no places to shower, the soup kitchens are horrible, and the criminal element is off the chain. Nashville was a tiny bit better, but not by much. They have a lot of issues there, too. Providence, at least, had Welcome Arnold. That's the name of their shelter. It's kept in the same complex as the penitentiary; kind of like a pleasant reminder to you should you stray off the course of righteousness. New York is just a scary place to live on skid row. You just never know from day to day if some deranged nut is going to run up to you and thrust some kitchen utensil between your ribs. It happens.

I think Seattle's reputation as a waystation for the homeless is growing. Every year they do a head count and the numbers are steadily increasing. But, bless their hearts, they are trying their best to eradicate the problem. One of the ideas they're looking into is studying how they address the problem in cities like San Francisco and Houston. The mayor recently hired a consultant from Obama's administration to help with the issues here even though I thought their money would've been better spent on sleeping bags and toilets because, after 9 months, the consultant will simply pocket the money and sail off into the sunset with her spanking brand new Escalade. Do you know what the consultant said a few weeks ago after having been on the job for 6 months? "Seattle has a homelessness problem." Really! Stevie Wonder could see that, Sherlock.

I'm trying to look at this moment of vagrancy in a positive light. Since I have all the time in the world to write, I'll write. When this book is done I'll proofread a novel I wrote a few years ago and publish it. After that, I plan to write a book of fiction called, "The Interview Book" or something like that. It'll be a collection of interviews I did with luminaries such as Beethoven, DaVinci, Mahavir, Mozart, Jesus of Nazareth, Mahatma Gandhi, Julius Caesar and others. I guess I should be grateful that I did, at least, study writing in school. It's paying off now that I have time. I suppose that's a plus for homelessness; I'd better not take it for granted.

***

I spent many weeks in the same QFC writing this book. Unbeknownst to me, one day, an older, homeless white woman sitting at a table behind me had me in her sights. As she got up to leave she walked straight over to me, glared into my eyes, handed me the following note, then left with the three or four large packages slung across her shoulders. Here's what it said:

"I am an author that works to stop all racist wars, to work for the cause of all people of color – yet why are you using certain leg positions that victimize me, also done most by white racist behind this war, against all people of color, blacks in particular. Doctors state those crossed ankle/leg positions and the shaking of legs cause severe swelling and pain in the legs of their victims – so ideally when I see you next – you will have to put a stop to it! Furthermore, I am an author and humanitarian, and have never in my life sold drugs – that is attempt on part of white racists to set me up for working in peace for Blacks, Asians & Hispanics."

Interestingly, this woman had impeccable, cursive penmanship as well as strong spelling chops. Why she chose to write to me is a mystery. I appreciate the attention, but now I'm nervous. I shake my legs all the time. Suppose she was sitting behind me another day and I wasn't paying attention? There I'd be, bouncing my legs up and down, then – bang! – she whacks me in the head with one of her bags. They *really* need to do something about the homeless in this town.

CHAPTER 39
Autism *and* Homelessness

"It is the shelter of each other that the people live." Irish proverb

You know, it's a deep dark shame. It is said that, in the general population, 1 in 88 people are autistic. That means, in your normal day of work or going to school or watching your favorite football team getting their collective butts kicked by their bitter rivals, one out of every 88 persons you see will be on the autistic spectrum. That's just a little more than 1% of the populace which, in all honesty, is still a relatively large number considering the headcount in America. In the homeless population, though, this number is ridiculous skewed. Here in Seattle, I swear, it's more like 75% of the homeless are autistic. What am I basing this number one? Well, either I just happen to get lucky finding a lot of autistic folks or, as they say, water finds its own levels, so maybe I was doomed to run into my own kind somewhere along the way.

It's just kind of twistedly funny, really. Because of the deep social disconnect a lot of us have, combined with our frequent comorbids like anxiety, depression and PTSD, it's near impossible for us to maintain employment, sustain positive relationships, keep our behinds out of trouble, get people to sympathize with the fact that, even though we may look like regular people, we're not. Physically we can blend in, but because of our unusual brain wiring, we may as well be from Mars. The bright lights and loud sounds of modern industrialized society turns some of us into slobbering cripples, making it difficult for us to navigate the morass of concrete and steel most people find as being unobtrusive in their lives. Crowded places repel some of us like mosquitoes circling a smoky campfire, too timid to take just one little sip from the bodies of warm blood just inches out of reach.

In essence, you'll often see autistics being divided into two camps – high functioning and low functioning. The high functioning ones blend in well in society, and unless they say what makes them tick, you'd think they were just simply odd or unusual in their ways.

The low functioning ones are more easily identifiable. Most are in institutions, some are non-verbal. Some are lacking in basic skills like feeding or dressing themselves. Some need redirection so often they keep their caregivers on their toes continuously. Generally, they are taken care of by the government, all medical and scholastic needs met by state-funded social service organizations. But when you think about it, which of the group of autistics are really high and low functioning? How can you be high functioning if your life is relegated to being out on the street 24 hours a day because, well, you just don't fit in well in society? The low functioning ones are having all their needs met. Theoretically, isn't that high-functioning while the homeless, tattered, loveless ones low functioning?

Today, you'll often hear people use the term 'Asperger's Syndrome', or 'Aspie', for short. Asperger's Syndrome was integrated into the autism category of the Diagnostic & Statistical Manual V (DSM-V) because the powers that be determined it was nothing more than autism-lite anyway. Basically, autism and Asperger's Syndrome are the same time, but from time to time, you will find that some aspies prefer to be called aspies to differentiate themselves from those who need more extensive hands-on care.

No one knows what causes autism but theories abound – alcoholic parents, childhood vaccinations, voodoo curses, punishment for misspent past lives, etc. Genetic testing is being conducted as we speak; pretty soon they'll be able to tell, in vitro, which child will be born with autism and which won't. Yes, this is bad news. Horrible news, really because, no doubt, babies will be aborted left and right by mothers thinking they're giving birth to Rain Man II. One so-called autism rights group, Autism Speaks, is leading the charge to identify and "deal with" potentially autistic babies. Autistics don't need a cure, we need understanding. A cure for autism is as ridiculous as a cure for left-handedness or homosexuality or red hair or brown eyes. We are what we are, dammit. Autism Speaks, deal with it!

Okay, just had to get that out of my system. Now, on to more pertinent matters – the roots of autism.

There's a popular idea currently circulating known as The Solitary Forager Hypothesis of autism. It purports to show that aspies were the discoverers, testers, frontiersmen, trailblazers and pathfinders of the Neanderthal/stone age era. Want to know if that mushroom will kill you? Just observe Og. He'll eat damn near anything.

The skills the early autistics developed over the years would be extremely helpful in a solitary environment but bad news when it came to being in a social group. For instance, this business about the lack of eye contact that some autistic folks have. In the wild, one animal staring into another's eyes is seen as a challenge, bad idea especially if the solitary forager is nowhere near as large as the animal they encountered. Heightened vision and hearing, annoying in today's noisy, confusing world, would have been necessary for survival in the past. Was that stirring in the brushes a few yards away simply the wind or a hungry predator? Acute attention to detail came in handy when determining if a plant or fruit was edible or poisonous. The spatial acuity some autists possess would've been helpful for finding their way around a large forest where danger lurked in every nook and cranny. And, of course, storing and categorizing items like food and wood would've been extremely helpful when the cold winter months hit.

Mankind, as he was evolving from his lizard roots, depended on the awareness of his amygdala and limbic system to keep him free of trouble and, by definition, alive. Later, the growing presence of the prefrontal cortex started to play a bigger role in logical reasoning. Is that animal coming towards me friend or foe? Your lizard brain would simply tell you to haul ass; your pre-fontal cortex would tell you to stand tall and investigate. Maybe the animal coming towards you has a different agenda, like fleeing a fire, chasing something else or just looking for someone to play with.

In the autistic brain, at least in some folks, there is a never-ending war between the amygdala and the prefrontal cortex. It's a constant fight for domination of the body. In neurotypicals, those without autism, their lizard brain, the ancient fight or flight machinery that doth exist, sits idly by while the normal vicissitudes of life transpire. In the autistic brain, the amygdala is like having spider senses, ever vigilant, ever responsive, ever surveying the environment for signs of danger. That hyper vigilance results in the high anxiety a lot of autistics possess, making it difficult for them to enjoy things normal people take for granted like concerts, shopping malls, discos, Black Friday sales at Wal-Mart, or any place where crowds of people assemble.

So, what can be done about the sheer number of homeless autistics in the streets? It begins with housing, supportive and permanent. Governments and corporations really need to invest in helping the poor just as they do with the Birkenstock-wearing contingent whose major turmoil is deciding whether to eat Creole-Grilled King salmon or Saffron & Dijon Mussels with frites at their favorite Cajun restaurant on a rainy Monday night. Remember, a happy pauper is one less pauper on a car prowl.

Medical assistance and, sadly, drug treatment, is often needed for the typical homeless autistic, too. I doubt any school child would say to themselves, "When I grow up I want to be a homeless addict in the street." That makes no sense. Because those with autism are extremely determined in their focus to accomplish whatever their minds tell them to, even if their sights are set on doing things of a negative nature, they will take it to fruition, come Hell or high water. It's very difficult to sway the thinking of the black and white, inflexible autistic mind. It'd probably be easier to get Cher to sing you a ballad that convince an Aspie to do as you say. All this stubbornness, of course, makes medically treating some people near impossible. It can be done but requires the patience of Job. But in the end, it's worth it. One less unstable person on the street for a safer neighborhood makes.

CHAPTER 40
Homeless Vegetarian Gumbo

"A homeless guy came up to me on the street and said he hadn't eaten in four days. I said, "Man, I wish I had your willpower."
Rodney Dangerfield, comedian

If you're like me, you eventually get tired of eating the same thing day after day, week after week, month after month, year after year – cans of cold ravioli, red kidney beans, spiced corn, pinto beans, Amy's exotic soups that, apparently, no one wants at Safeway, and bread so hard you can drive nails into stucco with them. And tuna. Cans and cans and cans of tuna. So much tuna you'd think there weren't any more left in the Pacific. Luckily, I do have an easy recipe to spice up your menu now and then, my Homeless Vegetarian Combo. Even your friends searching for butts and roaches in the park will stop and say, "Why, that's mighty fine gumbo right there!"

This is a recipe that's been in my collection for generations and generations, passed down by my great-great-great-great-great-great-great grand pappy, Oleo Resin, when he used to shoe General George Washington's horses. This version feeds four.

Ingredients:

2 bags (or cans) of black beans – you can obtain these in plentiful amounts from any food bank because, obviously, domiciled people don't eat it anyway as the supermarkets are all overstocked with them.

4 sesame seed crowns – The dumpster in the back of McDonald's always has Quarter Pounders that were thrown out because they stayed in the warming bin too long past their expiration time and Fat Johnny in checkout ignored them because he already stuffed himself with expired chicken nuggets.

1 bag of lettuce – Occasionally, Wendy's lays out way too much lettuce in their salad bars as if they were expecting a huge delegation of vegans to walk in from the convention center down the block. When they throw them out, use your foldable grabber thingy to pluck them out of the dumpster. Wendy's dumpsters, for some reason, seem deeper than others, making it difficult to climb in and out without being seen.

4 to 6 large potatoes – See below.

1 cup of Romano cheese – Taco Bell makes a side called Cheesy Fiesta Potatoes. Get about 12 packages of this South American goodness from their dumpster and you've got two ingredients right there. In case there are no Taco Bells in your neighborhood, the cheesy fries from Jack in the Box will do just fine.

1 bag of rice – Boiled or instant rice is preferred, but if you don't have an electrical outlet to plug in that old slow cooker your incarcerated friend left behind when he got snatched up for a parole violation last month, just let the rice you got from the food bank soak for six hours in cold water. You won't get that nice, white fluffy rice you're used to, but it's still edible and will sustain life.

1 cup of wine – Chardonnay or Riesling are the wines of choice, but if you're homeless, chances are you can only get your hands on MD 20/20 or Thunderbird. They'll still suffice. Just don't make noise when you boost it from 12-finger Tony sleeping in the bus stop across the street. If he has no rotgut, just substitute one can of Steel Reserve 211 or Olde English. Same difference. Of course, you can go really ghetto and do what I've, sad to say, done in the past – buy bottles of cooking sherry with food stamps and drink them like beer. Yeah, they're salty, and are probably a stroke waiting to happen, but at 17% alcohol content, they're good for a quick pick-me-up in the middle of a cold winter night.

1 cup of vegetable broth – Remember that field you were just relieving yourself in about 30 minutes ago? Guess what? Some of those plants you just watered were thyme, parsley and dill, maybe even rosemary. Just go back there, pluck a handful or two of leaves, and simmer them in 2 cups of water in a pot for five minutes or so. Instant broth. If you had already watered those plants before harvesting them, that's okay. You won't notice the taste. If one of your friends does comment on the "interesting" flavor of your gumbo, just tell them you used fresh ingredients, not the dried stuff from the food banks they're used to. Shopping malls have a lot of exotic plants, too. Maybe you can really spice things up by using some of those. I wouldn't, though, because I don't have the stones. Maybe you do.

6 ripe tomatoes – Food banks always have extras of these because the mushy ones they do have are so old they've started germinating already. Don't let the various thumb prints and black spots in the fruits deter you. Once they're cooking no one will notice the difference.

Place all the ingredients in that large steel pot those overweight campers from Wyoming donated last week and let it sit for five minutes. Dissect a skid, remove strips of wood, break them up into forearm-length stakes, and set them on fire in the park's rusty oven pit. After five minutes or so, place the gumbo on the grill and stir gently. You can use a spoon but I prefer a slat of wood because some of skids are made from hickory or pine and that adds a nice tang to the overall flavor. Add salt to taste then cover and let simmer for ten minutes. That's it. Spoon out a few bowls to your friends and watch them smile. Just so you know, if anyone gets sick, I'll deny the recipe came from me. Enjoy.

CHAPTER 41
Homeless Shelter Directory

"In today's climate in our country, which is sickened with the pollution of pollution, threatened with the prominence of AIDS, riddled with burgeoning racism, rife with growing huddles of the homeless, we need art and we need art in all forms. We need all methods of art to be present, everywhere present, and all the time present." Maya Angelou, poet, memoirist and civil rights activist.

One of the many places I was homeless in was SoCal, there from Cranston, Rhode Island in a brave attempt to write movies, hang out with Jack Nicholson and go skinny dipping in my soon-to-be-bought guitar-shaped swimming pool with Jay Chou (Kato from Green Hornet).Yeah, I know. Nothing spells excess like guitar-shaped pool, right? Why can't the pool resemble a potato chip or four leaf clover? Anyway, like so many hopefuls leaping off the bus at Hollywood & Vine, I dared to give L.A. a shot. Have you ever stood on the corner of Hollywood & Vine and watch the blonde starlets fly off the Greyhound buses with their naïve arms thrown up high in the air as to say, "Here I am!"? I feel so bad for them. They spent all their hard-earned money on bus tickets and acting lessons, sold their clothes, kissed everyone goodbye back in Podunk, Arkansas and rode for days to Hollywood just to encounter…silence. At the corner of Hollywood & Vine no one pays them any attention. In fact, it's so silent you can hear the hind legs of the L.A. crickets chirping out their plaintive tune, that perpetual soundtrack to the misbegotten and misguided.

Hollywood is like a giant carnivorous dinosaur. It can chew you up, eat you up, or swallow you whole. After it spits your bones out you're not recognizable anymore. Another one bites the dust. As fate would have it, I fell into a deep addiction while there. I became so despondent one night that I called the Suicide Hotline for help. Would you believe they put me on hold? That said, there's a glorious website for any downtrodden folks who need help. It's called Homeless Shelter Directory – Helping the Needy of America. This is their web address: http://www.homelessshelterdirectory.org/

Here is more about their directory as written on their website:

"The Homeless Shelter Directory provides Homeless Shelters and Homeless Service Organizations. This includes all resources necessary to help the needy. The Directory was created for people who want to find and donate food and/or supplies to their local shelter. Volunteer Opportunities are also needed at most shelters. I have listed contact information for volunteering at these shelters. Due to the current foreclosure rate and US recession, many shelters have waiting lists. Please call before going to the shelter." I pasted the following directly from their information page:

* Call the Provider Number listed on the all listing pages for help. Do not email the Homeless Shelter Directory for help. We are a website only. The Homeless Shelter Directory was started as a list of homeless shelters. We now provide listings for the following:

•Homeless Shelters
•Homeless Service Organizations
•Monetary Assistance
•Transitional Housing
•Free Clinics (Dental and Medical)
•Low Cost and Free Treatment Centers
•Outreach Centers
•Day Shelters
•Relief Organizations that can help the needy
•Women's Shelters and Battered Women's Services
•Food Pantries, Soup Kitchens, Food Banks

The Homeless Shelter Directory is pretty up to date and well laid out, so it shouldn't be a problem navigating through it. There's a convenient map on the main page that allows you to select specific states you're looking into. I wish this website had existed when I nearly fell to pieces in Hollywood years ago. Oh well, better late than never. Here are a few more useful numbers and url's.

National Suicide Prevention Lifeline – 1-800-273-TALK (8255). Use it for those days when you're down on your knees in the park saying to yourself, "Why me, Lord?"

Hopeline I'm Alive - http://hopeline.com/ You can use a computer to chat with someone there 24hrs a day. Their phone number is 1-800-784-2433.

Have a drinking problem? http://www.aa.org/ This Alcoholics Anonymous website will help you find meetings close to where you live, or not live, as the case might be.

Finally think that crack is wack? https://ca.org/ Give this site a visit to find Cocaine Anonymous meetings around the world as well as your neck of the woods.

Have a problem with other street pharmaceuticals? https://www.na.org/meetingsearch/ That's the link for Narcotics Anonymous where you can interact, face to face, with others struggling with addictions to opiates, shrooms, coke, meth, Molly or what have you.

Is MJ your drug of choice but find she's too difficult to ignore? https://www.marijuana-anonymous.org/meetings/find You can thank me later.

For those of you who'd rather be around folks that use China White, Black Tar and Horse: http://www.heroinanonymous.org/ They'll point you in the right direction.

Here's a club whose only requirement for membership is a desire to stop using Crystal Meth: http://crystalmeth.org/ I've been seeing more and more meth (or Shabu as they call it in downtown Manila) users on the street and, according to the news, it is a worldwide epidemic.

For you non-using family and friends of addicts, have a look at this 12 Step Program: http://www.nar-anon.org/ Through them, you can find a meeting, get literature, the latest news and other items.

Seeking a 12-step fellowship of men and women helping each other live nicotine-free lives? https://nicotine-anonymous.org/

Some people would rather go to secular meetings than those which are religion based, and that's fine. http://www.sossobriety.org/ Secular Organizations for Sobriety has been around for 31 years to help addicts and alcoholics recover. They have meetings all over the world.

The U.S. Department of Housing and Urban Development also has homeless assistance resources for your particular residential or urban area, whether you are in the shelter or street. http://portal.hud.gov/hudportal/HUD?src=/program_offices/comm_pl anning/homeless

If you're a homeless veteran call the HUDVET National Hotline at (877)-424-3838.

Need a Social Security card? The Social Security Administration link to finding an office near you is: https://secure.ssa.gov/ICON/main.jsp Or you can call 1-800-772-1213.

You can also get a new or replacement Social Security number and card online (for those days when the shelter clerk says, "Sorry, no card, no bed). https://www.ssa.gov/ssnumber/

Need an ID? State-issued cards for you non-drivers are necessary to get into transitional housing, subsidized housing or even regular housing (should you hit the jackpot someday). Here's the National DMV office finder link: http://www.dmv.org/dmv-office-finder.php

BTW, if you're as poor as Michael Jackson after a lawsuit, your local DHS/DSHS can give you a form for getting a reduced fee ID from your local DMV office. The prices I've seen usually hover around $5 or $6. You just go to your DSHS' Community Service Office, get a Request for Identification form completed by said welfare office and take the whole kit and caboodle to DMV or Department of Licensing as it's called in Washington.

U.S. Dept. of Health & Human Services. Now, here's a pretty comprehensive site. HHS oversees programs and services that improve the well-being of individuals, families and communities. On the site, you can find out how to get temporary financial assistance in your state or area, food stamps (SNAP program), Head Start, Foster Care, Programs for Persons with Disabilities, and of course, information about grants, research and resources related to the homeless. http://www.hhs.gov/programs/social-services/index.html

Sometimes you absolutely, positively have to get issues off your chest or you'll burst into flames. I'm not saying that contacting Congress, whether local, state or national will garner you a response, but if it'll help you sleep at night knowing at least somebody has heard your point of view, here's the link. http://www.contactingthecongress.org/ There are phone numbers and email addresses aplenty. Remember, be courteous, avoid words that would make a sailor blush, and if they ask you who put you up to it, I'll categorically deny it was me.

So, there you have it in a nutshell, You Can't Sleep Here: A Clown's Guide to Surviving Homelessness. Being down and out in the streets is a bummer, a real buzz kill, but it can be done even for a long time. Hopefully, the two big takeaways you got from this guide were 'have hope and persevere'. Just hang in there. It can be done. If you have to say that to yourself over and over again till you believe it, go ahead. You. Are. Not. Alone. Remember the great French writer Alexandre Dumas? He wrote The Count of Monte Cristo, The Three Musketeers, The Corsican Brothers and the Great Dictionary of Cuisine (good ol' Alex was a foodie). I'll now leave you with one of his quotes and hope it brings great inspiration to you.

"There is neither happiness nor misery in the world; there is only the comparison of one state with another, nothing more. He who has felt the deepest grief is best able to experience supreme happiness. We must have felt what it is to die, Morrel, that we may appreciate the enjoyments of life. Live, then, and be happy, beloved children of my heart, and never forget, that until the day God will deign to reveal the future to man, all human wisdom is contained in these two words, Wait and Hope."

My sentiments exactly.

***

ACKNOWLEDGEMENTS

"Yoga is the most boring exercise. It's for people who are too lazy to get on the elliptical. Bikram, where they heat up the room to mimic India's climate, is especially stupid. People in India are not skinny because they're doing yoga in 105-degree rooms; they're skinny because there's no food." Noureen DeWulf

I placed the above bit on yoga at the edge of this acknowledgements page because I thought it was insightful as well as funny. One of the stupidest comments I've received from people is I should do yoga – it'll help me out with my homelessness. It will? You mean sitting in a lotus position for hours will get me a studio apartment at the high rise of my choice? I beg to differ. All meditation will do is annoy me to death and prolong the fact that, after I wake up from imitating a pretzel, I'll still be eating Chef Boyardee cold right out of the can in a public park somewhere.

At this time, I'd like to acknowledge all the people who do go out of their way to help the homeless in any possible fashion they can. I once walked barefooted, through the rain no less, into a local Value Village thrift store. The used sneakers on sale there cost $12. The manager came along and said, "Take whatever pair you want and just walk out the front door." Really? Just like that? I had to check his badge just to make sure I wasn't being set up. So I quickly donned the pair (Italian Superga's – never heard of them till then) and bounced, looking over my shoulder for the police. Well, that was nice of the manager. I still thank him to this day.

Recently, the night clerk at a local 7-Eleven felt sorry for me because it was freezing outside, so he went out to his car and gave me a black, puffy Michael Kors jacket. It's in really good shape, too. He said his sister had just had it dry cleaned. You know what's odd, though? The night clerk doesn't talk to me anymore. In fact, it seems like he outright hates me. I don't know why. I've walked in the store drunk on a few occasions, but it's not like I was being obnoxious, destroying the place or boosting stuff. Maybe he has me mixed up with someone else. As you know, all we homeless people look alike, so maybe that's the reason.

I've received free clothes from a hospital, too. Of course, I was as naked as a jaybird when I walked in, but that's another story for some other time. I'd also like to thank the lady with the pitbull who's come by my car a few times and gave me food and drinks. Very nice of her. We need more people like that in the world. I'd also like to thank the folks who inadvertently leave me money in the mall parking lot as well as sunglasses, cans of soda, shoes, socks, and other miscellanea. It's helped me to keep my head up, thus preventing thoughts of leaping off a bridge from entering my head.

***

OUT *of* PRINT TITLES
The Robin
I'm Not a Carpet
Scream with the Rhythm

Those three out of print books I'd written in my juvenile years were released on Sound Off Press from Ames, IA back in the 80's. I make it seem like a big deal, but I owned Sound Off Press. As a matter of fact, it wasn't even a real publishing house. I was a student at Iowa State University and, when I discovered the campus Kinko's bound books, I created my own titles. I do have a cute little story related to those books though, particularly, *Scream with the Rhythm.*

Back in the day, the City of Mt. Vernon, NY had an acting school that was run by Tina Sattin. Tina was a good friend of mine so I once brought *Scream with the Rhythm* for her to read. About two weeks had passed and I figured she may have plucked through a few pages already, so I went to the studio to ask her about it, and take it back since it was the only copy I had. When I got there, I didn't take the book because someone was reading it at the time, Denzel Washington. I didn't want to interrupt him so I just let it be.

That was 30 years ago. I wonder if Brother Denzel remembers those days? Eh, who am I kidding? I'm just a homeless dude. Respect is as elusive to us as Steven Seagal's Academy Award. Denzel, if you're reading this, and you have *Scream with the Rhythm* in your possession, can you return it? You know what? Don't. My writing was probably so juvenile back then I'm sure I'd cringe at what I wrote. Never mind, Denzel. Thanks, anyway.

Made in the USA
San Bernardino, CA
07 September 2017